Devil's Avatar

DENISE SNOW

DEVIL'S AVATAR

**ANOTHER
PERSPECTIVE FOR
ADDICTS AND
THEIR FAMILIES**

Two Harbors Press

Copyright © 2012 by Denise Snow.

Two Harbors Press
212 3rd Avenue North, Suite 290
Minneapolis, MN 55401
612.455.2293
www.TwoHarborsPress.com

All rights reserved. No part of this publication may be reproduced, stored in a retrieval system, or transmitted, in any form or by any means, electronic, mechanical, photocopying, recording, or otherwise, without the prior written permission of the author.

ISBN-13: 978-1-937293-69-7
LCCN: 2011943113

Cover Photo © 2011. All rights reserved - used with permission.

Distributed by Itasca Books

Cover Design and Typeset by Nate Meyers

Printed in the United States of America

Dedication

To Kelly's friends, who tried to help her, and whom she loved; and to all the medical professionals who tried their best.

Contents

Introduction xi

1. Ingredients for Disaster–ADD Personality 1

2. Puberty 11

3. Should Have Been Stricter 17

4. The "Innerspacegirl's" Files 23

5. Notes on Parents and Closest Friends 33

6. Post High School and College 43

7. Valley Hope 55

8. Sierra Tucson 61

9. After Rehabs 73

10. The Army Idea 85

11. The Roller Coaster Years... 101

12. The Dark Year, 2010 121

13. Leftover Evil 135

14. Finding the Files 137

15. Trip to Portland 141

16. Final File Entry, January 2005 145

References... 151

Avatar – \'a-və-,tär\ noun
2. b: an embodiment (as of a concept or philosophy) often in a person

"avatar." Merriam-Webster.com. 2011. http://www.meriam-webster.com (1 August 2011).

Introduction

Christmas is probably the worst time of year to have a death in your family. Our only child, Kelly, died right before Christmas 2010. She was 25 years old. We had two stacks of cards going: one for Christmas from the early senders and the other for condolences. Friends were calling to wish us Merry Christmas and we freaked them out with the news. I know we joined millions of people in this surreal experience up until the part where we disclosed that her death was from a drug overdose. Suddenly the paradigm shifted and went into under-drive for some people we had considered friends or at least good acquaintances. The word was "mum," that is to say, we heard not even one word from them.

I'm sure the circumstances of Kelly's death made them uncomfortable and they probably thought silence was their best tool to make it all go away. It could also be that some people thought Kelly was "bad" because she used drugs and, thus, her death didn't deserve recognition. And then there were the friends who knew what had just happened and still gave Christmas cards wishing us the merriest Christmas ever without a word about Kelly. In any event, as parents who went through so much anguish, it hurt to not even be recognized as suffering at least the same as other parents. It was a final insult delivered by the evil of drug addiction.

Through our ordeal, we have learned many painful lessons. To tuck them away in some far recess of our minds and not share them with others just coming into our same boat would be unconscionable. During Kelly's journey of destruction, there came a point of such darkness that my husband and I felt we had been given a clarifying message. I don't know what to call it. Was it an actual revelation? An "epiphany"? I don't know. But it came way too late in the battle, and too late for Kelly. At the point in time when we realized what was going on, there was no communicating with her about such things anymore. The message was this: All the known treatments, therapies and rehabs are important aspects of drug and alcohol recovery, but that is not the level where the real battle is fought. We were at war with a primary force: evil. Never was this brought up to us directly, so that we could clearly see its truth, although it was hinted at in subtle round-about ways. Even if it had been clearly presented, we would have automatically dismissed any spiritual aspect of Kelly's addiction problem. That would have been "crazy talk" and not helpful—perhaps even wasteful of our precious time—when we were facing a real-life crisis. In words that could easily have been ours, "Leave us alone with that crap. We have a *real* problem here!"

Honesty was the biggest hurdle we had to overcome in order to reach the truth about addiction. Unfortunately, it was hard to be frank and open with others and our-

Introduction

selves about things that hurt, embarrassed, or scared us. We helped it thrive; it was the easy way. Eventually there came a point in time when the years of pain from watching Kelly sink to her demise had numbed us and honesty was able to come easily and quietly to us. The clarity was overwhelming and the truth was simply there for us to believe. If you are in the darkest of places, where Kelly's cognitive dissonance nightmare took place, you can feel it yourself that something is wrong—bad wrong. Don't throw an instinct away because it may seem silly in its unexamined state. In our case, we noticed that everyone connected with Kelly was in some way sucked-in or affected by evil—people, who we would never have expected (including us), did inexplicably bad things. Why? Something was going on—something so far out of our paradigm that we couldn't comprehend it.

When Kelly was ten years old, our family attended a Catholic First Communion mass for the daughter of friends. The priest warned the communicants about the Devil. He said evil is real and Satan is real and that the children were never to play with tarot cards or Ouija boards. I remember Kelly, my husband, Doug, and I giggling away in the car on our ride home. *How archaic! How could a late 20th century person say that with a straight face?* Well, we're not laughing anymore. The priest knew back then what we had to learn for ourselves the hard way. There most definitely is a force called Evil; my family had to get slapped by it to believe it. I'm not so sure if I believe the other things, but I wouldn't tempt fate at this point, either. Someday I will tell that priest he was right and that we "get it."

I left all the thorns and bark on Kelly's story because it is the hard truth. Real addiction stories aren't pretty and most don't end well. No one wants to tell you this because it doesn't seem helpful to rob you of your hope. The truth gets leaked to you in small doses during rehab and by therapists. What we needed at the time we first learned Kelly was addicted, was a BIG slap of reality right up front. We deceived ourselves with the idea that things weren't as bad as they seemed. Yes, they were; she was in deep trouble. Things got so bad that it even became clear to us only God could save her. I remember Doug and I talking about divine intervention at one point as our only hope. If Kelly had been spiritually oriented, it wouldn't have to have been a passive thing: waiting to get saved. She could have fought for herself to win her life. Unfortunately, she didn't know where the battlefield was. If you are not religiously oriented, as we weren't, you probably will have a really hard time coming to grips with this. We learned where the last stand—the fight between good and evil—takes place and are passing this information on. If you are lucky enough to have a solid spiritual foundation, you already have your primary weapon. If you don't, you have a little harder path, but you can still get rid of any preconceived hang-ups and try to believe that there might be something to this.

I wrote Kelly's story using a metaphor centered around the Devil in order to put a face on the concept of evil. With this in mind, think of drugs as the Devil's poison and the user becoming his "avatar." Once he takes hold, his evil spreads like cancer. Slowly at first, and then more rapidly, until the drug user and all in the user's web of associations become victims, in some way, of this primal force. Towards the end, the drug user actually loses his soul. The person who used to reside in the body is gone and only the Devil piloting his avatar on a joyride

Introduction

remains. Eventually the avatar itself destructs—flesh and blood can only sustain so much abuse before the organs collapse and the brain shuts down. The family members are then left to mourn the person who used to be their kin as they bury the Devil's abused and discarded play toy.

As parents, we didn't know what we were facing or how to proceed. We learned as we went. If you have been on your own addiction journey through living hell, you will know that unless you or your loved one stops using, there are only three outcomes for the drug abuser: prison, institutionalization, or death. When prison or institutionalization starts to look good to you, we will already be kindred spirits. There are many of us family members of addicts, and we are automatically fellow travelers. Shame ensures that we are usually silent about our suffering. I have learned, however, that if I have the guts to mention it, all kinds of people, who I never would have guessed, will tell me they've also been affected by addiction in some way. I think we battle-worn warriors actually become better people through living the nightmare, but at an impossible price. We no longer make snap judgments about others. We come out the other side of that "know it all" tunnel very different people. The word "mensch" comes to mind. "Walk a mile in someone else's shoes" is our well-worn mantra. People who have been through this wringer have a stoic acceptance of the human condition. It's a kind of "inverse blessing."

We only had one child. Our marriage has been stable and happy and our home was pretty calm. Neither of us has ever had substance abuse problems, we are educated, had no financial problems, and both grew up in good homes. This was the first big lesson we learned and it hit us like an atom bomb: Nothing is for sure. Never think the outcome of your lives or your children's lives are in your control. There is a reason so many in the world say "God willing" before they begin a sentence. Arrogant people like us with no bumps or hardships in life are the ones who are the most prone to thinking all they have to do is make a plan and execute it well, and nothing will go wrong. Imagine the power of that lesson for us, when everything was planned and went completely wrong. Nothing is ever "for sure." We were traveling along "la-di-dah" in life one day, and the next we found ourselves sucked into a ten-year journey through every circle of hell.

Kelly left 51 journals chronicling her life, including her journey through mental illness and drugs. After she died, we retrieved the journals from a storage unit in Portland, Oregon. I can only write about what we went through from a parent's perspective. Her side of the story remains concealed in her most personal journals. She would never forgive us for reading them. I would never do it, anyway, because I don't want to know what is in them—it would hurt us too much. But I consider her files and notebooks fair game, though they are still worrisome enough to me about crossing the line of personal betrayal. They lend enough insight on their own into what happened, and into how a girl who had everything ended up losing it all. If only we could have known the things we read in those notebooks and files early on! They tell how, when, and why she took a wrong turn. Then again, maybe it wouldn't have made any difference at all; maybe our fates are sealed from the outset. I came to believe that nothing she could do would surprise us, yet she always managed to do just that. Kelly's frenzied artwork, her collages, and her single-minded pursuit of stand-up comedy tell us she had a lot of chaos going on in her head. Drugs,

Introduction

illegal and legal, gave her a false sense of relief, but they only added another layer of disaster to her life. In the end, the drugs destroyed her mind and her body.

What I think about the most when I read some of the writings Kelly left behind is how aware she was of the destruction drugs were doing to her life and our lives, and how much she had to live for, yet how unable she was to unshackle herself. For some people, only one taste of drugs is needed, and they are forever hooked. Their craving for more and stronger drugs defies logic as they inject, swallow, or snort and don't care that they're careening toward death.

Kelly's story tells us just how powerful drugs are. No matter how bright your future is, or how bright you are, once ensnared you will go down and you will take a lot of hearts down with you. I hope Kelly's story and the avatar allegory will provide a way for you, or a loved one, to see what's going on from a different perspective and help you win your battle.

CHAPTER 1:
Ingredients for Disaster – ADD Personality

The magnetized photo frame sticking to our refrigerator holds a photo of Kelly on the day of the Rodeo Queen contest. The year was 2000 and she was fifteen—with long blond hair, loose and curled, a giant smile debuting her newly-aligned teeth, and a fresh happy face. For the next ten years it would be the only photo of her I displayed. It clings to the refrigerator door, Janus-like, marking the end of her innocence and the beginning of her end. The photo freezes in time our only child on the cusp of taking the most destructive wrong turn of her life, from which she could never recover. It wouldn't be until three years later that we learned she had become a drug addict, taking her first sample around the time of the photo. In every picture of her after that, I sensed something wrong with her looks and demeanor, though I couldn't put my finger on what exactly was bothering me. I blamed her new vegetarian diet and the fact she was in the middle of her teen years. This was surely a phase, and I thought I would just wait it out until it was mercifully over, then put new photos up. Kelly would say, "Mom, I hate that photo. Why do you only keep that one up?"

I gave her the same answer each time, "Because you still looked healthy then and you were eating *our* food." I hoped this would end her un-researched pseudo-vegetarian phase, in which she fed herself peanut butter and chips. Though we hated our powerlessness, we accepted it as just another case of Kelly being Kelly, which had become completely normal for us. We didn't recognize that, in actuality, she had a whopping case of Attention Deficit Disorder (ADD). Behavior that other parents may have thought odd didn't alarm us, because we had grown used to it over the course of her childhood.

Because she was our only child, we couldn't compare her to a sibling. We just accepted her as a bright and happy kid who was extremely energetic—and what my parents' generation would have called "a handful." I stayed home because I knew she needed me. If we had trouble handling her, how could we expect another person to do it who wasn't at least related and compelled to care about her as we did? Whatever was going on with Kelly, we only saw her unique personality and we were absolutely certain she would mature out of most of her parent-trying behaviors. Besides, there were two of us for one child—surely we could handle the challenge! She was a fun little kid with a twisted sense of humor and a goal of becoming a comedian some day. Her sheer exuberance and bright spirit cancelled out any worries we had. We were the proudest parents in the world.

In the early 1990s, when Kelly started going to school, not many people knew what ADD was, including us. We had heard about it but, from what we could tell, it was something that affected boys who were very hyperactive.

Chapter 1

Kelly wasn't a boy and we didn't consider her THAT hyperactive, so we didn't bother to read much on the subject. If ever there was a fork in the road that we wish we could go back to and change directions, that was it. Kelly had every symptom of the disorder: problems with impulse control, attention, and hyperactivity. She was unaware of the consequences to her actions, couldn't focus, would race from task to task, forgot and lost things, was easily bored, and craved excitement and stimulation. In people with ADD, the frontal lobe of their brains lack activity (this is what's known as "Hypofrontality"). In simple (very simple) layman's terms, all the brain parts are there, but the "secretary," who normally organizes, coordinates, and runs an orderly office, is away from her desk. A person with ADD just can't seem to ever "get his or her shit together," for lack of a better description. (See the reference section for an actual explanation by a doctor.)

Kelly had to learn every lesson the hard way and, in many instances, over and over again, often never learning them. There was no listening to us because everything was "boring." If she had a decision to make, you could bet she would make the wrong choice every single time. All through her growing years we would have to grab her from stepping out in the road if she saw someone or something of interest on the other side. In fact, she was hit by a car and ended up hospitalized with a severe concussion and a broken hip when she darted across a street after a neighbor waved to show her new kittens. This was ADD's curse of impulsiveness and lack of self-control. There was the time when she suddenly let the shelter dog off the leash while we were volunteering, the time we rented a video camera for an hour and she wasn't paying attention and dropped it within ten minutes, the time... (I could go on and on.) Our pets and her horse understood what was going on better than we did. They stayed out of her way because she was unintentionally hard on them. She wasn't able to recognize when they had had enough handling; she simply couldn't control herself. Kelly loved animals, so I know this hurt her.

Our dog died when Kelly was six. This somehow triggered her to dance on desktops in her first-grade classroom. The school counselor called us in and told us he had given an IQ test to her and determined Kelly to have an IQ of 142. He said that, ordinarily, this would have allowed her to jump to the third grade, but that in her case, she was simply too immature. There was no mention of the possibility of ADD, although that would have been a good time for someone to bring it up. The professional assessment for Kelly's behavior was "immaturity" and everyone knows the cure for that is time. Besides, we were proud of this confirmation of how smart she was.

But, if she was so smart, then why did we have to tell her the simplest things over and over again? "Kelly, don't walk through the house with muddy shoes. Don't fill your glass so full that the drink spills all over the floor. Don't lose the house key. Don't brush so hard with your toothbrush, etc." My husband, Doug, and I were frustrated and we translated her behavior as meaning that she did not care about us, her parents. We looked back on our own childhoods and remembered how we cared about our family and especially wanted to please our parents. We couldn't help wondering if maybe she just didn't love us. After she died, Doug and I cleaned out her apartment and found the carpet covered with tracked-in dirt and coffee spill stains from her over-filled cups. All the keys to the apartment were lost and we threw out her last toothbrush

Chapter 1

with smashed bristles that day. She had never been doing those things *to* us. It was never about us. Kelly was just unable to jump over her own shadow.

"Easy" is the word we knew was plaguing Kelly. She looked for the easy way out for everything. Most of the time, the easy way led her to failure, yet she never stopped trying to push the easy button. Many were the times she wouldn't study the patterns for a horse show event, choosing instead to socialize and joke around. Even after losing those events and, therefore, the coveted ribbons and competitions, she still repeated the same behaviors. She would complete homework assignments but not bother to turn them in, thus losing credit. We were frustrated with her because this would happen over and over again. Deep deep down inside, we were afraid. How could she manage her life with this going on? And then we would go back to the comfortable place in our heads that kept telling us not to worry, because she would grow out of it all.

Respecting money was another problem for Kelly. When she was eleven years old, Doug signed up for program called "Parent Banc" with our insurance company. The idea was to give kids a checkbook and bank account (backed-up by the parents, of course) with a limit to what could be withdrawn. It was a way to train kids to be responsible. After Kelly's first trip to a mall with some girls, she had the whole account drained. This complete inability to handle money never changed during her whole life. We could never give her more than a few dollars in cash because it would disappear, and she was always in debt and overdrawn at the bank.

By the time she was in the eighth grade, I had Kelly signed up—at one point or another—with just about every extracurricular class available, in the hope that one of them would spark an interest in her. She had been introduced to ballet, cheerleading, skiing, ice skating, roller skating, tennis, golf, piano, gymnastics, guitar, pottery, photography and horseback riding lessons. Nothing ever really interested her enough to stick with it, except horseback riding. The stables had a 4-H program and, thus, she had a built-in circle of girlfriends. This aspect was very attractive to her because she had a really hard time keeping friends. Though Kelly was gregarious and full of fun ideas—like having a horse wedding and keeping a younger pair of boys at the stables as "slave boys"—there were constantly conflicts with other girls. Kids were initially attracted to her, but her lack of self-control would drive them away in short order. In the early days, when Kelly was in first or second grade, I even used to befriend other mothers of girls her age so that she would have playmates. I held parties for no reason other than to draw in the kids. Once the parties were underway, Kelly would whip herself into such a wild state that we would have to send everyone home telling them it wasn't their fault, our kid just couldn't control herself.

Clues were coming in from other people that maybe there was something going on with Kelly—more than what was "normal"—but everything rolled off us like water off a duck's back. "Crazy" was the adjective some of Kelly's friends were using with her name, but I never thought it was meant in a mean way. I'll never forget a group of kids approached me asking if I was Kelly's mom, at an open house meeting of Kelly's 7th grade class. They wanted to tell me how they always joked about Kelly's parents and how sorry they felt for them. I thought it was funny and appreciated the acknowledgment of our super effort as good parents. Another time, a horseback riding girlfriend

Chapter 1

of Kelly's told me innocently that her dad said he was glad Kelly wasn't his kid. Well, I thought, I was glad she wasn't, too. These comments bothered me on a subconscious level, or I wouldn't remember them as I do.

Like many girls in their early teens, Kelly became a vegetarian. We worried about her health and our family life, but she loved animals so much that she thought it was immoral to eat them. I told her that I didn't like doing it either, but we humans are omnivores and need meat. I was proud of her for taking a stand and sticking to it with such firm conviction, even though I fought against her vegetarianism for health reasons. We made her go to a doctor who gave her blood tests. In retrospect, for our family life, I should have stepped-up and cooked special vegetarian meals, because she didn't want to come to the table with us anymore. We missed our opportunity to see her and talk to her every day. (Big mistake. Huge.) Our strategy to "wait it out" was dumb; she stayed a vegetarian until she was 23. We gave her vitamins to help make up for missing nutrients, and it turns out she was throwing them away because they were brown. She told us later she thought they might be poison. I couldn't believe she would think such a thing! She just laughed, saying she was a "weird kid." This was disturbing on the obvious level, but reassuring in another backwards kind of way. At least we knew Kelly would not be one of those kids who messed around with drugs; she was way too fussy about what went into her body. I have to admit that, armed with this false sense of security, we didn't talk at home about the dangers of drug experimentation as often as we should have, as it seemed such a remote possibility.

Then came the big day of the Rodeo Queen contest. Kelly was first runner-up. She could have won the contest had it not been for her old nemesis, ADD, and her new nemesis, drug abuse. Both were present to screw up her life then, and over and over again afterward. Kelly won the horsemanship portion of the contest and the presentation of her platform to the judges. In fact, she was in the lead. But, in the final crucial segment of the competition that evening, in front of a packed hall of cowboys, she entered the stage to the tune of her favorite musical selection: the silly 1960s-sounding theme song from "Austin Powers." No common sense, no fear of consequences, no impulse control and no telling Kelly anything. (Hello, Kelly! R-o-d-e-o. *Western* music.) Nobody was able to talk her out of it. The judges also advised her not to slouch, and to stand up straight—something that had never been a problem before—and I couldn't understand why it was becoming one. She didn't listen to them, either.

For the past eight years I have been writing off and on in my "sort-of" journal. When I reread my notes, I told my husband that I could not write this book because people would think we were absolutely the stupidest parents in the world. Looking backward, we did so many things wrong. He answered that I should still do it, because it is part of the story. Which parents out there are perfect? How do you know when mental illness steps into the picture? What kind of discipline and structure are the best for which type of child? If you don't know something, then how can you recognize it and guard against it?

As a mom, I tried to help Kelly by guiding her. I would always tell her "don't do this" or "don't do that." I checked out books and videos from the library on teaching kids proper manners and such. I looked at my job as making sure Kelly reached college and would survive in

Chapter 1

life. Kelly saw my hovering as smothering. She thought I was critical of her and "projecting my own failings onto her." I have a German mother; Kelly didn't know what critical was.

I don't believe I was critical, but I often had to check Kelly's behavior and steer her in a better direction. This turned into a bad cycle. The more I tried to help, the more she did the opposite of what I suggested. By the time she entered puberty, we had a pretty dysfunctional relationship. Worse yet, I did not know it was dysfunctional.

What I can impart to someone else whose child exhibits ADD symptoms, up to and including the problems Kelly had (such as no fear of consequences, no common sense, an inability to focus on a goal or task, no self-preservation button, and a high sense of self-confidence at least on the outside), is that he or she is going to have a hard road through life. The worst thing that can happen to complicate treatment or amelioration of these conditions would be to layer another quagmire such as addiction over all the rest of the problems. Once addiction gets added to the mix, you can't work on helping the person develop the survival skills she'll need to lead a productive life until the effects of drugs or alcohol aren't clouding her brain. As my family learned, only a small percentage of people manage to conquer their addiction, as it is one of the most difficult challenges a person can face. The key, of course, would be to prevent that moment of first encounter with the Devil's poison, because an ADD personality is likely to love the newly discovered false sense of victory over their problems.

CHAPTER 2
Puberty

From being the smallest kid in her eighth grade class to developing a full-fledged double-D cup by the tenth grade, Kelly hit puberty with a bang. It's too bad the changes in her body didn't come on more gradually, giving her a chance to adjust to the new social circumstances into which they thrust her. She wasn't mature enough to handle all the new attention she was getting; it came way too fast. During this same time, she was winning jumping awards at regionals in 4-H and became president of her 4-H club. She was in the high school's speech and debate club and the drama club. She was the center of attention in a lot of ways which were new to her. When she lost her interest in horses all of a sudden and stopped caring overnight, we just thought it was because of boys. Other mothers had told us this could happen. We were bothered, though, by how completely she shut off her interest in her horse, not even going to visit Lady in the barn fifty yards from our house. We chalked all of this up to puberty and being a teenager and knew Kelly was going to give us a run for our money before she eventually came around.

In the tenth grade, Kelly was searching for new friends because she didn't fit in the little clique of religiously oriented girls she had been hanging around with at that time. Kelly told me that she didn't feel like she was like other kids. I told her that was nonsense and gave her the "everyone is unique" speech. I wish, now, that I had really listened to her concerns. I told her she just needed to make different friends than this super-religious bunch. Soon afterwards we moved away from the city into our new home in a national forest area. She complained that, by doing so, we ruined her social life. We told her a lot of Army kids move all the time and that she'd be fine. Looking back, this move was the wrong thing to do.

No sooner were we in the new house than the new set of friends began showing up. These were polar opposites from the religious girls. One had purple hair, and the other wore mismatched socks and looked like the cat had dragged her. We told Kelly to find different friends. We knew that when teenagers have a change in friends, especially to weird ones, it was a warning sign. However, Kelly had an entire lifetime of difficulties with friends and we were sure she would soon lose these as well. We also had a sense she was smoking marijuana. We didn't catch her, but she was acting strangely. We confronted her and she admitted to it and said she just tried it like all the other kids. (I did the same thing in the tenth grade.) We gave her the lectures and warnings and were glad when the new friends disappeared.

In the eleventh grade, Kelly's grandmother gave her a 2000 VW Beetle. My mom thought she was doing a nice thing because Kelly could now drive herself to school and

Chapter 2

take the burden off of Doug each morning, but after that, we hardly saw Kelly. She had a best girlfriend, whom we really liked, and that friend spent the night sometimes. She also had a slightly older, responsible, girlfriend from the 4-H club. Kelly claimed we lived too remotely for friends to drive all the way out, causing her to hang out at their houses. She was very smart and knew better than to break our rules (home by six on school days, and home by midnight on weekends). She called to tell us where she was and had to drive across a military fort twice a day to get back and forth to school. There never was an incident with the gate guards or military police to give us a warning by arresting her for driving poorly, being "high," or confiscating drugs from her car. There was never anything like that. Granted, her grades weren't what they had been, but they were still in the As and Bs with some Cs. Though she had been in the "fast track" program all of her elementary years and through middle school, by this time she was only in two honors classes. To be honest, we were glad she was fitting in finally and had a clique. After all those years, she was coming into her own finding friends. Her social skills were much improved and she seemed to be thriving. I always thought that consideration of others was not something that came naturally to her; she had learned what worked and what didn't by then. Fitting in with friends was a big improvement.

At the same time, some things were happening that alarmed us. Kelly was coating her bedroom walls with magazine clippings. From top to bottom, and on every wall, was a giant collage of weird pictures. She said this was her self-expression and we let it go at that. We had lived in military quarters most of her life and had never allowed her to mar the walls; it was only fair to let her have some freedom in her own room. I do recall asking her why she didn't stop adding pictures before the collage became so cluttered people couldn't understand the picture. She answered that she only stopped when a collage was "done" and she knew exactly when that was. Every item in her room was painted with squiggles (in permanent paint). (Oh well, teenagers!) In tenth grade, she asked us for filing cabinets for her birthday. It was a strange request, but we were glad she was going to be responsible and file.

We caught Kelly stealing money out of our wallets. When we confronted her, she cried and apologized and said she was using it to buy posters. We believed and forgave her even though, after writing this, I finally realize that her room was covered in collages—why would she need posters? A neighbor called me one morning and said he was just passed on his way to work by Kelly speeding.

Okay, it was time to send her to a psychologist/therapist, we decided. This was new territory we were charting. We didn't know anything about therapists and just picked a name out of the phone book. New lesson: never pick a therapist out of the phone book. This woman was ready to retire in a month and was obviously burned-out. She saw Kelly a couple of times and then had one session with Kelly and me together. Her advice was telling Kelly not to speed and relaying a story about how, in her church, they have a ceremony where the new drivers get handed their car keys—or some such thing. Needless to say, that was a waste of money and soured me on psychologists. I am sure now, though, that Kelly never mentioned anything to that woman about drug abuse.

Chapter 2

The last semester of Kelly's senior year she was so snippy and moody that we frankly couldn't wait for her to go off to college. We never got the feeling that Doug, her grandmother, our family pets, her discarded horse or I mattered even slightly to her. I secretly wondered if she might have had a detachment disorder. Some people told us that this was normal and that in a few years she would turn back into a human like their kids did. We figured, at that point, we'd let her college roommates tell her off—she wouldn't listen to us but she would listen to them. Her grades were now Bs and Cs, even a D. We worried that she might not even get into college, so we signed her up for a seven-day SAT prep course in Tucson, which, she later confessed to us in rehab, she ditched most of to "punish us for making her go." Somehow Kelly still managed to get a decent score and was accepted to the University of Arizona.

To sum it up, Kelly was an enigma. She was a narcissist, yet had deep insecurities and low self-esteem. So well did she cover up the latter, that we never even knew she had those feelings until she told us her resentments in rehab. She was extremely happy, yet there was a sadness that she never reached her potential. Smart, yet she had no common sense. Lazy, but she was wild and energetic when sparked. She wanted more of everything, but died protecting only her most important possessions: her journals and files. She was disorganized and chaotic, yet a filing maniac. A good person at her core, but she was easily able to behave badly.

We worried how our daughter would survive in the real world when she left the nest. Her lack of common sense didn't bode well. The most elementary survival skills, like dealing with money or not walking out into the street, just weren't there. She would need good friends who would replace our function of watching out for her. We wondered if she would find such friends since she had a way of pissing most potential ones off.

ADD in this extreme is life-threatening, as Kelly's short life proved. She simply didn't have the full set of skills to manage life. On the other hand, she was extremely bright, engaging in wit, and attractive. People were drawn to her, unfortunately among the nice ones were many predators who found in her an easy mark. We had to let her leave the nest or she would have just run away.

From that day when we brought Kelly off to college and she spun around yelling "I'm free! I'm free!" her life was never safe and secure again.

CHAPTER 3
Should Have Been Stricter

The following are things Doug and I did wrong while raising Kelly. Some things were totally our fault because we should have been stricter, and others were unwittingly our fault because we simply didn't have the knowledge or experience to know what we were seeing:

- Allowing Kelly to have a car was a big mistake. So what if she lived remotely; we should have been tougher. Period.
- We should have snooped in her closet or in her purse. I never liked the idea because I grew up in the post-WWII years when the connotations of "Nazi" and "Gestapo" were well imprinted in my head. Kelly wasn't breaking any rules, and I didn't think I should invade her bedroom like that. Too bad we don't get a second chance.
- We should have made a bigger effort to meet her friends. She told me only about her "good" friends

(who didn't do drugs). The good girlfriends were the ones who came and spent the nights. Only two boys ever came over to our house once or twice and they didn't stay long, which was fine by us. We had no reason to assume there were probably a lot more bad friends than good ones. She told us nobody would drive out 45 minutes to see her and be bored to tears, so she spent her time in town at the mall or at her friends' houses. This was another mistake, but one I didn't know how to manage at the time. We had horses and work to do at home and I couldn't be following her around after school. Keeping her home alone would have been an undeserved punishment, based on the information we had. We should have checked-up on her much more closely, to follow the old adage "Trust, but Verify."

- We should have known better than to think a person with certain characteristics in childhood will lose the ones we don't like (lack of common sense, impulsiveness, etc.) while maintaining the ones we do like (funny, kind, good-natured, etc.) when she grows up. Such thinking isn't rational, except during childhood and puberty when changes happen all the time through the process of maturing. Sometimes people don't mature and they don't change.

Things we didn't do anything about because we didn't know what they were:

- Some strange toys or decorations were appearing in her room. One was this "silver clacker ball thing" with balls suspended by strings, which would keep clicking the balls once you snapped it to start it. We just

Chapter 3

were disgusted that she would waste her money on stupid toys when she seemed too old for such things. There was a lava lamp. We thought it was part of her "Austin Powers" phase, which was reasonable for us to think since our dog, Austin, and her guinea pig, Scot Evil, were named after characters in the movie. We found out, later that these "toys" enhance a meth or drug experience. (File this in your "good to know" file.)

- She had a bad smell about her during the winter of her last school year. We kept the house closed up to keep the heat in, so we noticed her bedroom, her bathroom, and her person smelled like rotting onions. I couldn't wait for her to leave for school and for the chance to air the house out. I never associated the smell with meth use. How would I have known that those were connected? I thought she smelled like onions because of her vegetarian diet. It's a delicate thing to tell a teenage girl she stinks, and the last thing I wanted to do was give her a complex, so I told her to cut back on onions. Sometimes, when I changed her sheets, there were these strange brownish gooey crystal-ish streaks on her pillow case. I couldn't even imagine why they were there; I wondered what would make smears like that. I wondered if it came out of her mouth or nose or was it just crud that got on her pillow. The best I can surmise from an internet search is that it could have been hashish resin, but why it was on her pillow case (at least twice), who knows? Maybe I should have asked her, but she would have just lied. In rehab, later, she told me that she was delighted I had given her the excuse about onions so she didn't even have to make up her own lie.

- She was sick a lot. This was always a hard call for me. When is a kid lying and when is she really sick? She certainly *seemed* sick. That she was hung-over from drug abuse didn't even register in my mind.

Things you don't know because you don't know:

- ADD and Bipolar disorder. We had no idea what they were, only that we seemed to be having much more trouble raising our kid than other parents had with theirs. (See the summary of ADD and Bipolar Disorder in the reference section at the end of the book.)
- Being lied to and deceived. If you don't lie and you don't know anybody who lies, then chances are you won't recognize lies, especially if they are skillfully delivered. Kelly was truant and tardy many times in her last year of high school. After she died, we found a file full of pink slips from the school office, which we had never seen. On the bottom of the slips the following were listed for copies: "White to Office, Yellow to Teacher, Pink to Student and Gold to Counselor." There was no "Copy to Parents." Shouldn't we have gotten one? We never knew she was in trouble for skipping classes and Public Displays of Affection (PDA) at school! The school called a few times to confirm that she was sick at home, but they never called us in to talk to a counselor. When Kelly had detention, she just told us it was for academic reasons or minor transgressions like talking in class. Even so, those times that she was given detention weren't known to us since she drove herself home. In short, never underestimate what a smart manipulative kid

Chapter 3

is capable of doing. The more gifted the kid is at manipulating, the less you are going to realize what is occurring.

- Bad Posture. We couldn't figure this one out. Starting around puberty, Kelly began hunching her shoulders. I would poke her in the back between the shoulder blades with my knuckle whenever I noticed, so she would straighten up. Her bad posture bothered me immensely because I didn't understand why she couldn't correct it. (How difficult is it to stand up straight?) I knew she could do it, because whenever she rode her horse, she had no problem at all (a throw-back to all the years of training for horseback riding competitions). She was such an extrovert that I never thought of her as having insecurities and, thus, I spent the next nine years sticking my knuckle into her back, pissing-off both of us in the process. I wish someone would have given me the following advice: "Bad posture is a red flag. There is something wrong—something making the person feel self-conscious or inferior. It could be nothing more than a pimple or bad hair at that age, but if you can't see a physical reason, dig deeper!" In a way, having such a red flag would have been a blessing, because it betrays the shame and guilty feelings deep down inside, despite any clever cover-up kids on drugs can deliver. (Of course, someone who doesn't have a conscience won't have this problem.)

CHAPTER 4
The "Innerspacegirl's" Files

Although I can't bring myself to read Kelly's journals, I did read her files and other notebooks. A sad story was revealed to me through them. There was so much going on in Kelly's head, but our communication had deteriorated so badly through her puberty years that she didn't come to Doug and me for help. The persona she presented to us was that of a supremely confident happy teenager. She added an exclamation point after her name and used it until the end of her life, despite our protests: "Kelly Snow!" If she could have gotten it to blink on the page, she would have liked it even better. We thought "Great! Our kid is going somewhere in life." I was happy she had the self-confidence I never had. On the other hand, the name she gave herself for her email address was "Innerspacegirl." Without any reason to suspect an irony, we thought it just sounded clever, like everything Kelly created. Looking back, how could we have missed that? "Kelly Snow! The Innerspacegirl."

DEVIL'S AVATAR

The following entries were in the Twelve-Step journal she kept at a halfway house a year and a half after high school graduation. (The Twelve-Step Program is the primary tool for recovering addicts in which they follow a set of guiding principles leading to a course of action. Along with acknowledging they are powerless over their addictions and recognizing their "Higher Power," addicts must examine their past transgressions and make amends so they can move on with their lives and start again with clean slates.) It was during this process when Kelly wrote her resentments and deepest feelings. I share them because maybe someone out there will recognize the pattern of insecurity hidden by an overwhelming show of confidence and happiness. Kelly's reality was split like the Greek masks for comedy and drama. I'm sure if some good could come from disclosing what was in her notebooks, Kelly would forgive me.

> *Tom Janson* (Grade 10)
> *1) Introducing me to drugz/drug culture.*
> *FEAR: getting into it F'real and getting hooked*
>   *- saying no and not trying it out*
>   *- saying no and getting peer-pressure*
>   *- getting in trouble*
> *SELF-SEEKING: I expect a good relationship with someone I know to be high.*
> *I wanted status with the drug kids without risking my other high school relations. I knew what it was all about, I liked it and I wanted more*
> *DISHONESTY: I said yes without hesitation*
>   *- I lied to my friends about the nature of the relationship*
>   *- I befriended lame people for free drugz*

Chapter 4

2) Getting me into my first real trouble by getting two "referrals" for PDA (Public Displays of Affection)
   - my parents were ashamed of me and angry
FEAR: My parents' disapproval
   - peer assumptions and social slander
SELF-SEEKING: I want to have my fun and not be ashamed.
   - I don't want a "slut" label
   - I don't want negative disregard from my parents.
I didn't say no—I made out and went along with it in spite of my dislike and grossed-out peers. (takes 2 to PDA)
DISHONESTY: I lied about my trouble to mom and dad
   -I never set a boundary with Tom

3) Convincing me to ditch, steal, litter, smoke, get high, lie, make out in public, and engage in all of the other behaviors 10th graders are susceptible to.
FEAR: sinking to his level
   - losing my morality
   - being guilty of everything my parents would be ashamed of.
   - being a dork in front of Tom
   - peer pressure, insecurity, being "bad" in my own eyes.
I allowed myself to do it and was enthusiastically eager to pick these behaviors up.
DISHONESTY: I didn't put up any moral resistance and instead pushed my own boundaries despite my reservations inside.
SELF-SEEKING: I want to be accepted, a cool girlfriend, naughty, and rebellious without moral damage.

Reading her words, I knew that, right then and there was the moment of infection. A new avatar had been welcomed into the fold. When that boy gave her the first drug, it was like the first taste of the apple that drove humans out of paradise. It was Kelly's first drink of the Devil's elixir allowing him inside to caress the control panel of his new avatar. I'm sure that, at that point, he was dreaming of the evil he could do using a beautiful young girl's body. It must have been like taking candy from a baby considering her insecurities and problems.

However, Kelly did put up a fight, at least for the next four or five years. She was tormented and tortured in her fight for morality. She did have decency deeply embedded in her soul. Even so, drugs, the Devil's poison, would addict her body and consume her brain—a fight she could never win. I am sure the fight was an intoxicating challenge for the Devil, and that the evil he spread to everyone Kelly touched was a thrill.

> *Tina Simmons & Co.* (She was the mismatched socks girl when Kelly changed friends)
> *Using me and "bringing me down" in high school, morality, motivation, drugs, and personality.*
> - *using me for cash, drugz, rides, and stuff she didn't pay for.*
>
> DISHONESTY: *I lied to my parents about who my friends were.*
> - *I made up stories to sound more hard-core to the kids.*
>
> FEAR: *being a loser.*
> - *having to make new friends.*
> - *not having any of the fun I was used to.*
>
> *I knew I was involved with the wrong people and didn't break away.*

Chapter 4

SELF-SEEKING: I felt "better" than these trashy people.
   - I want to be cool and start partying.
   - I expect to be in the "in crowd" with any crowd.

High Ravers
   - showing me a mirror of myself in my most vulnerable state
   - being sloppy, irresponsible, dumb, and hard to deal with.
FEAR: my world being tried in front of me and knowing it.
   - trusting high ravers
   - self-conscious fear of being watched by not-high ravers.
SELF-SEEKING: I don't want to be who I was, I don't want to be looked down upon by the sober kids, I don't want to associate with people like myself.
I got more high at raves than most of the partyers there.
I fit my own resentment to a T.
DISHONESTY: I hid my distaste while I was practicing myself.
   - my friends were all high ravers.

Crackheads/junkies
Scamming me, stealing my money and CDs, following me, expecting a reward for hooking me up. Resembling me.
I interacted with these people by choice and high-ambitions
FEAR: becoming one.
   - having one steal or lie to me.
   - Competing for drugs and having paranoia about being ripped-off.

DEVIL'S AVATAR

> *DISHONESTY: I've ripped people off too.*
> *SELF-SEEKING: I want to do drugs and not become what everyone else does. I'm different.*

I wonder if the curiosity about drugs might be particularly piqued in a kid who comes from a home where there is no experience, or even thought, given to something so remote from the family's life style. I know we didn't discuss illegal drugs as much as we should have with her, assuming they would be as alien to Kelly's mindset as they were to ours.

In the eighth grade, Kelly's Honors English teacher gave the class an assignment: "If you could do anything you wanted for a day without consequences, what would it be?" Kelly's paper was on taking drugs to see what it is all about, but without consequences and having her brain ruined. She got an A. At the time, I looked at her paper as "just another A" on an English assignment. Now I wish that teacher had given her an A for grammar, but had made a point by giving her a non-recorded F for a really bad idea. I think we all need to bump up our adult influences when we have an opportunity and ram home the "drugs are bad" lesson every chance we get.

Kelly blamed D.A.R.E., her town, and her school's assistant principal, but knew in her heart it was her own fault.

> *D.A.R.E.*
> *Giving me the initial curiosity about drugs and wasting everyone's time, tax money, and evoking more curiosity than prevention*
> *FEAR: Listening*

Chapter 4

- hearing propaganda go to kids
- being wrong
The DARE program only gave me anti-drug information and I sparked my own inquires.
DISHONESTY: I mistook the information provided and knowingly placed blame.

My Town, AZ
Being the worst possible place for someone like me to grow up in.
Housing an ambition-sucking vortex and my high school
FEAR: never being able to leave
   - having my roots in a place where I hate most institutions and attitudes
   - being "less" than people who can succeed in my town
SELF-SEEKING: I am spiteful and uppity
   - I blame surroundings for my problems
   - I think negative first
I created all of my problems and town-distortions around my shortcomings
DISHONESTY: I am willing to blame my shortcomings on a force far outside myself.

Mrs. Summers (Kelly's high school assistant principal)
1) Not showing mercy in calling my parents when I got in trouble for embarrassing stuff.
FEAR: my mom knowing the things I did to soil my record and bring shame to myself.
*PDA referrals.
   - the trouble that would come as a result of my mom hearing from Mrs. Summers.
SELF-SEEKING: I don't want to accept consequences

DEVIL'S AVATAR

> *- I don't want my mom to frown on me.*
> DISHONESTY: *I lied to my mom when I'd say I didn't know about the things Mrs. Summers would phone home about.*
>
> *2) Coming after me meticulously and calling me in for ridiculous shit.*
> FEAR: *getting caught for drugs on account of some petty hallway violation.*
> *- having this administrative bitch come after me. I had a lot of bad behaviors to pick on.*
> *Perhaps I have created this assumption in my head.*
> DISHONESTY: *I created this resentment to take blame off of myself.*
> SELF-SEEKING: *I don't want to be responsible for myself and she made a good target of an authority figure.*

The following is about the mother of one of Kelly's friends (which makes me have a resentment of my own, now).

> *Samantha's mother*
> *1) Prying into <u>my</u> business and making passive-aggressive threats to call my parents if Samantha continues to hang out with me.*
> FEAR: *getting caught.*
> *- Samantha's mom looking lowly upon me.*
> *- my parents getting me in trouble: Being aware of my deeds*
> *- not getting to chill with Samantha*
> SELF-SEEKING: *I do not want Mrs. Davidson in my affairs because she may be right and I feel bad doing the same thing to two sets of parents.*

Chapter 4

> *I got myself into the things she is against in the first place.*
> *DISHONESTY: I lied to her about a lot of things I later was nailed for.*
>
> *2) Searching Samantha's room and grounding her for drugs that were "obviously" mine.*
> *- Putting guilt about it/her feelings onto me.*
> *FEAR: getting in trouble for more than my part.*
> *- feeling wrong getting her into trouble.*
> *They were my drugs; I was, in part, responsible for Samantha's problems.*
> *DISHONESTY: I denied the knowledge of any stash.*
> *SELF-SEEKING: I don't want to be bad, caught, responsible for Samantha or responsible for my own actions.*

Why didn't Samantha's mom call us? We parents have to grasp how bad drugs are and network with each other. It's a form of evil to NOT tell another kid's parents for something this dangerous! This is but one more example of what I mean by saying that addiction has a way of sucking everyone connected to it into its vortex.

CHAPTER 5
Notes about Parents and Closest Friends

The following resentments from Kelly's Twelve Step notebook were about Doug and me. I have included all of them, so that nobody can say I skipped ones I didn't like. After I read these entries, I felt heart-broken. Hindsight is 20/20. The patterns stick out so clearly. All that time Doug and I were angry because she was misbehaving and lying to us, we could have been helping her had we only known. It was a vicious cycle. The more she felt badly about her drug use and moral slide, the more she used drugs to feel better. The more drugs she took, the more her grades went down and the more she behaved badly and got into trouble and lied, and the more we criticized or "tried to help" (depending on your viewpoint). The less we praised and hugged because we were angry and frustrated, the worse she felt about herself compared to how she "should have been" and how her sober friends were and how their parents were treating them.

My Mother
1) Offering me "helpful" superficial advice and commentary about my clothes/hair/make-up, etc.
FEAR: I am inferior, defective, wrong, ugly, fat, mismatched, dumb (...etc...) and my mother knows it but I do not.
DISHONEST: I told myself that I was all of these things if my mom made negative comments to me.
I want only positive regard because my self-esteem is fragile and my mom's opinion means a lot to me.
SELF-SEEKING: I wanted only good comments, good regard, and nice remarks from my mom to boost my ego. Instead I got a third party objective view and had my ego deflated.
  - her opinion is very important to me and I am hurt by any comment intended to be taken lightly.

2) Giving me a hard time about becoming a vegetarian and pressuring me to eat the way she does by manipulating and punishing me.
DISHONESTY: I didn't tell anyone that I secretly got a kick out of putting my mom through vegetarian frustration and I liked knowing that she had no power over my "ethically-based" diet.
FEAR: I would lose power over my body, beliefs, and self-will. My mom would hold a lot of control over me with food.
SELFISH: I expected her to go along with my new belief without putting up a legit argument for my health.
SELF-SEEKING: I wanted what I wanted, how I wanted it and I didn't expect anyone to argue.

3) Emotionally manipulating me (crying, yelling, using animals/people. Playing victim, etc.)
DISHONEST: I label every good fighting tactic of hers as unfair so I don't have to look at myself.

Chapter 5

FEAR: I will have to look at myself instead of putting more blame and anger on my mother.
SELFISH: being more angry about that behavior pattern than I am about what I did to deserve it.
SELF-SEEKING: I don't want to be mean, bad, or wrong, so I reverse arguments to hurt my mom instead.

4) Not going to/balking at attending little ceremonies at schools or clubs. Not attending events that she thought were dorky and not wanting to talk to other kids' parents at such functions.
FEAR: Missing out on my peers' activities.
  - *mom would think I'm dorky.*
  - *not being a part of some "rites of passage."*
  - *having an antisocial mom—everyone else had social ones.*
SELFISH: I downplayed my desire for her attendance because I didn't want to be dorky, but I also never stood up, agreeing instead.
DISHONEST: I never told her "please come" and feigned "too cool" attitudes. I told other kids that I was way too cool for shit I really wanted.
SELF-SEEKING I wanted mom's attention and positive opinion of me. I expected her to be like other moms.

FATHER
1) Not expressing emotion towards me or my accomplishments.
FEAR: insecure of my dad's approval of me.
  - *not knowing him REALLY.*
  - *miscommunication.*
  - *alienation/estrangement.*

DISHONEST: I embellish and attempt to manipulate his emotional responses so I can get the reactions I want.
Often times I expect certain comments or reactions and feel disappointed when I can't read him.
SELF-SEEKING: I seek approval, my parents' pride and deep internal positive regard.

2) Never hugging, kissing, or making physical contact with me.
FEAR: My dad disapproves of me.
   - my dad is angry or distant.
   - I am not fully validated.
   - my layer of security-blanket is not on.
DISHONESTY: I expect him to initiate hugs on his own.
I never seek closeness from him and feel jealous of kids with "hugger-parents."
SELF-SEEKING: I want more emotional comfort than I know my dad will provide.

3) Distrusting me.
DISHONEST: I lie.
   - I expect them to trust me.
FEAR: rejection, not getting privileges or acceptance.
   - being wrong or honest
I broke a trust we established often and took their trust for granted.
SELF-SEEKING: I don't want to work to build a relationship or earn trust when I habitually tell dad lies.

4) Making decisions for me.
FEAR: Being spoken for.
   - losing power.

Chapter 5

- not getting to do what I want.
- being walked over.
- trusting his good judgment.
DISHONEST: *I don't admit when he's right or when I need his help.*
I make poor choices and put him in situations where I can't help myself.
SELF-SEEKING: *I want my way and the easier/more fun illogical way when I know my dad is/could help me.*
  - I dislike authority.

5) *Being critical and less appreciative/more judgmental about what I do instead of telling me what I SHOULD be doing.*
FEAR: *disapproval*
  - not ever being good enough
DISHONEST: *I embellish the good and avoid the parts I feel will put him off when I share.*
I only want to hear praise and resent a lecture/criticism.
SELF-SEEKING: *I don't want his opinion or his practical advice. It is a bitch to listen to and I seek praise.*

6) *Using his childhood values as a framework for the rules imposed on me.*
  - expecting my morals to be the same as his.
FEAR: *not being good growing up like him.*
  - being ethically inferior.
  - letting my parents' expectations down.
DISHONEST: *I lie, too.*
I don't follow their moral code and expect not to get scolded when I am wrong.
SELF-SEEKING: *I expect morality to work the way I want it to and don't want to handle consequences.*

We didn't raise Kelly the way she was behaving and I suspect she must have had these feelings of guilt and shame because of the internal conflict. Did she realize she wasn't being hugged because of her behavior, or was she behaving like this because she wasn't hugged enough?

I will always feel badly about this cycle. It hurt to read her words, since we wanted nothing more than to be closer to her. It is too bad we couldn't have just sent notes to each other, if talking was the obstacle. It's heartbreaking to know now, after it is too late, that all we both ever wanted was the same thing. I wish I could go back in time, have her back, and hug her like she craved. It was hard at the time to hug a little monster, but I wish I had my little monster back. We loved her so much; we couldn't even imagine she wouldn't know that.

> *My Best Friend, Miles* (There were 12 entries—I'm only using #5 and #10.)
> *5) Never saying no to me or my ideas—being weak with boundaries or Kelly-proofing."*
> *FEAR: Having to control myself on my own*
>   *- not having a scapegoat/alibi*
>   *- not having the smarter party outside control on my behavior that I am accustomed to in my friendships.*
> *DISHONEST: I never allow him to take decision making initiative*
>   *- I make excuses for myself.*
> *I expect to be told no to ideas that I can't stop myself from wanting to act out on, but I expect Miles to put his foot down for me. He never does.*
> *SELF-SEEKING: I want good bad fun with no consequences to be personally responsible for.*
>   *- I don't want to make all of the decisions.*

Chapter 5

> *10) Putting me into situations like when his mom called me for help and advice and truth to use against him.*
> *   - telling me to lie to her to keep him out of trouble.*
> *   - catch-22 - Narcing me*
> *DISHONEST:*
> *   - lying to his mom downplaying the truth*
> *   - withholding information about where he is/what he's doing if she calls me.*
> *   - not telling Miles the extent of my disclosure when he needs to know what she knows.*
> *I don't set a boundary about what to do in the event of a "Where is Miles?" pop quiz.*
> *   - I lie to his mom sometimes.*
> *   - I don't tell him what I say to her.*
> *FEAR: Miles's mom won't like me and I'll feel guilty for supporting his lie.*
> *   - Miles won't trust me and will think I'm backstabbing.*
> *SELF-SEEKING: I want both of them to like me and to please them with what they want to hear, so they won't be mad at me.*

I can just picture Kelly writing the above about Miles and his mom—it's so "Kelly." She never wanted to hurt anyone. Since she had no internal control over her behavior, she had to rely on others to apply the brakes for her. Miles was so smitten and desiring to please, that he would never say "No" to anything Kelly wanted. They were inseparable friends, but a disastrous combination.

> *Yeem - (The older girlfriend Kelly looked up to)*
> *1) Jealousy. Not being able to resent Yeem.*
> *FEAR: being in second place*
> *   - not having attention*

- feeling bad and inferior
- being under the "care" of a person so far removed from the lows of my disease.
SELF-SEEKING: *I don't want to be <u>less</u> or feel <u>less</u> than my friend and roommate.*
- I get a backwards kick out of projecting my morals onto her actions and seeing the right/wrong dichotomy.
- She is busy, skinny, beautiful, fun, honest, responsible, sober, studious, artistic, fashionable, employed, supported by proud parents, and she has self-esteem without arrogance. {JEALOUS}
I allow myself to idealize Yeem and to resent her for being "better" on the whole than me.
DISHONESTY: *I don't want to pick flaws in her because of guilt.*
- I tell myself how opposite Yeem I am.

Julie (Kelly's best girl friend)
1) JEALOUSY: *I resent her for everything she has better than me.*
FEAR: *Being the bad seed*
- being inferior as the dominant half of a friendship
- being insecure of myself
- handling jealousy while being so close/friendly to her
SELF-SEEKING: *I do not want to be the shadow of Julie.*
- I am jealous of her for: Being beautiful, being effortlessly beautiful, being humble, being innocent in her actions and talk, being <u>thin</u> by nature, picking up qualities of mine that she projected better, taking over my friendships/boys, not doing drugs like me, being moral and perfect and her parents adore her.

Chapter 5

> *I want what I do not have and belittle or idolize what I cannot be/have.*
> *DISHONESTY: I believe what I imagine to be real about her and fathom that I will never be it.*

Had I not been forged—through this whole process of the last ten years—into a more tolerant and merciful person, and if I were reading all of this so far about someone else, I would probably be thinking right now: "What's the matter with those people? How could they be that stupid? What was the matter with that girl? She should have just said 'NO.' How easy is that? She was just a spoiled brat. No self-discipline. The parents weren't strict enough."

But guess what? There is something else working here and most people don't even know it exists. The Devil has a very powerful weapon in his arsenal called "Denial." It is equivalent to the Air Force's "Bunker Buster" bomb. With denial, the horror of the truth is so unfathomable that you can't even see it—so you are unable to acknowledge it. You won't peel off the layers of obvious clues, because you don't—no, you CAN'T—bear the truth. Your mind actually shuts out information that can damage your psyche, in the same way that a person in an accident goes into shock.

People have a built-in "normalcy bias." We just want everything to be "normal." Kelly was our only child. All of our dreams were wrapped-up in her welfare—her future being safe, happy and successful. Each clue that she was taking a wrong turn from that path was not making it through our screen of denial to us. It's a phenomenon that is hard to comprehend, but it is a major problem in dealing with drug abusers and their loved ones. Imagine how strong this denial weapon is when you consider the fact that most drug addicts and alcoholics (or addicts of any sort) truly don't believe they have a problem. You can't even begin meaningful treatment until there is recognition.

We learned about this in family week at rehab and still didn't see ourselves! In fact, so strong is this "blocking defense of the mind," that neither Doug nor I remembered until we were writing this that Kelly did bring out a box from her closet with drug paraphernalia when we confronted her in 10th grade. I am remembering other clues now that should have tripped the alarm bells at the time, yet—at the time—we blanked-out on them.

Armed with the confidence afforded to people who have never been in someone else's shoes, it is easy to judge us. I know, because we used to be like that ourselves. Now I always think about walking a mile in someone else's shoes before I judge.

A weird thing is happening to Doug and me because of all the crap we've been through for the last ten years. Despite ourselves, we are turning into nicer people than we were. (It's sure a hell of a way to get there!)

CHAPTER 6
Post High School and College

We made Kelly get a job at a local supermarket during the summer before her first semester at the University of Arizona. We thought it would be good for her to see how hard money is to come by. All it did was make Kelly resent us, and our relationship with her, more than ever. To be honest, Doug and I were tired—worn out. I hate to admit it, but I couldn't wait for her to move to college and begin turning into a human again, like our friends promised would happen.

Kelly moved into a house near the university with Yeem, her responsible friend who was two years ahead of her, and another girl from the 4-H horse program. It wasn't three weeks into the first semester before she met a 28 year-old guy at a party. We learned of this through a family friend about our age, Markus, who was sort of like an uncle to Kelly. He would keep me informed of what Kelly was up to, because we had no decent communication with her anymore. The problem with this set-up was that Kelly was lying to Markus, too. Markus informed us that the new boyfriend was 24; we were mortified. He also told us Kelly had gotten a tongue ring. *Gross! Disgusting! Druggie-like! We put two sets of braces on that kid and now she goes and beats-up her teeth with a tongue ring!* This was too much to bear!

Shortly after that, Doug and I received the following "smarty pants" letter from Kelly; I suppose it was her attempt at adult communication with us. It only upset us:

> Mom,
>
> *I've been puzzling over your letter to me for a couple of days now, and I know we need to have a big blowout of unpleasant things before we can have a resolution and get along as parent and child—but as adults. We tend to do that best with writing, as it takes the ego-battle out of our arguments. That's why I'll mail this to you old-school style instead of sending email.........*
>
> *I'm informed, I'm aware, and I'm very happy with my current situation. These things are so awkward to tell you about, but I hope our relationship will improve now that you know.*
>
> *Secondly, I always assume that you always assume that I'm doing drugs in some way or another. This is a touchy subject even to suggest in our household, and I know we will never agree about it.*
>
> *I have not, will not, and am not using your money to buy drugs. This does not sit with me morally and I know it is the LAST thing in the world you or Dad want anything to do with. I screwed you over in this department in the past and I never want to do that again. So I am not.*

Chapter 6

However, as a parent and as a Republican, I know you don't want me to have anything to do with drugs anyways. Mom, I've seen what substance abuse can do to people firsthand and I know I don't want to end up that way ever. My viewpoint on occasional recreational marijuana use obviously won't settle with you...I honestly do not believe it is wrong. At least not for me. I've done the research and I know the risks and I've found a way to balance these things so as not to jeopardize my brain or safety if I occasionally smoke pot in a social situation. Mom, there is nothing you can do about it...just know that I'm aware of the dangers and I take them very seriously. I like my brain and my body. Quite a lot.

As far as other drugs are concerned, I try to avoid most of them and the people that abuse them. Since I've moved here, I've used three times (mushrooms, LSD, and ecstasy) and I do not regret any of them. Once again, these are things I hate to tell you, but if we are being open, then I think you should know.

My experiences were very enlightening to me. I know what I want to do and what I have to do to get there. I am aware of things beyond my self-absorbed self and the little universe that surrounds me. I can't begin to tell you the changes that have happened inside of me, Mom, you wouldn't understand.

I weighed the potential consequences and took all the measures to control health, legal, and safety hazards. I knew exactly what I was getting into and I couldn't be more satisfied with the result. These experiences I wouldn't trade for anything and I am a better person for having had them.

DEVIL'S AVATAR

We will fundamentally disagree on this issue forever, but I hope you feel better for knowing the truth. I have made responsible decisions for myself about a serious issue, unfortunately these are not the decisions you would like me to make, sorry for that.

Your primary concern for me is school, and I have told you and told you and tried to show you how I am doing and you do not believe me. I go to class every day and do my homework every night and study as much as I need to. Once again I will relay to you that I like college. I intend to finish it and will enjoy the process of getting to that point because I WANT to learn the things I am learning. I don't want to keep repeating this to you, so I hope you will listen to me this time and I won't have to.

I'm working hard. It is completely different than high school and my attitude toward it is completely different, too.

You will always obsess about my health and there is nothing you can do to impact it except telling me what to do. [deleted discussion of her vegetarian diet] I want a healthy body and complexion and you don't need to convince me to want them. Please stop.

(Oh, there is so much I need to cover in this letter and I'm getting tired writing it.)

I'm sorry about the big bank overdraft. There is nothing I can do about it now, but it was completely irresponsible of me to write checks and use my debit card without keeping track of the balance. I had no intention of spending anything that wasn't there and especially not causing you and Dad the trouble and ridiculous compensation of funds that I did. Under the

Chapter 6

new system, that won't be a problem. Ugh. This is one part of real life that I haven't caught onto yet. Sorry, sorry, sorry.

In conclusion, living on my own has made me a completely different person and I think I have a handle on how the world works now. Whether or not you agree with some of the decisions I have made for myself, I want you to know that they have been informed and well thought out. I hope you can respect me as an adult for this. I'm on my way to where I want to end up and we need to resolve our issues in order for me to get there.

I love you so much, Mom. I don't want to hurt you, but I'm sure some of this has. This is the beginning of our reshaping our relationship to each other and one day I wish you will be my friend. I think you will like who I've become outside of being just your daughter. Please don't worry about me. I'm very happy and on my way to perfect balance and self-actualization. That's how I am doing, how are you??

Love,
Kelly!

P.S. I worry about Dad's reaction to a letter like this. Perhaps you can give him a warning before passing this over.

That was one scary letter. You can almost feel the Devil dictating it verbatim to his new avatar. It was in Kelly's handwriting, but it's obvious that he had the controls. Just a little note to let her parents know how much fun he had been having with her. His poison elixir of drugs and alcohol had allowed him to pull his oldest trick on her: making her believe she knew everything, like she was her own God. "I have everything in control and I have the tiger by its tail" is the signature of a drug addict in big trouble.

Doug answered her letter in an email we saved:

November 18, 2003

Kelly,

Tonight I finally read the letter you sent Momba. I put it off this long as I was trying to avoid the pain it would bring me. I was wrong to do that to Momba. I was right about the pain it brought me.

First, your drug use, no matter how enlightening you imagine it to be, must stop. Your claim of being in control is the same belief every drug addict starts with. You have a hard time controlling your spending and telephone use. When you are taking drugs you are not in control. How can we believe you can control drug use? How can you actually believe that? Is this how you define being an adult?

The quality control of what you take is, of course, on your side. How do you control this? It's a game of Russian roulette. Remember, the geniuses in that trailer are really concerned about your health and have never made a mistake in their concoctions—you can get their guarantee on that.

We will not fund your bad, illegal behavior. You say you don't use our money to pay for drugs, so where do you get the money for them? You will become beholding to those that give you drugs as no one gives

Chapter 6

them away without expecting something in return. No matter what is stated, anyone that sells drugs does it to make a profit of some kind. The more they sell and the easier you can make it for them to do so is all the better for them. No one who engages in this business really likes themselves because they know that what they do destroys lives. Hang with those of this crowd and you will ensure an ugly, painful existence. It's not an issue of if, but one of when.

Expect to have unnecessary contact with law enforcement. It will not be at all like getting a speeding ticket. For many that contact is what it eventually takes to get a grip on what's important in life, to realize the hard way that drugs are not part of that. And then there are the losers.

You demand that we just accept you this way. We don't. We have demands, too. Our demand is that as long as we are paying your way we will not accept this behavior. You are on a path of destruction that we will not be part of. Your behaviors are directly counter to your success in school.

Lastly, I am glad you told us all this. I too wish that we could better communicate with you, but am not sure how that is possible as long as you maintain that everything must revolve around you and your wants and demands. It's time to be the adult you say you are.

Love,
Dad

About a month after that letter, around mid-December 2003 when Kelly came home for Christmas break from school, we asked if we could see her report card. She said report cards weren't ready yet and that they would only come out in January. Looking back now, I realize that was a lie but we bought it at the time. After all, by college, parents shouldn't have to talk to the school staff and teachers. Then she asked if she could see a psychiatrist. We wanted to know what for, and she said she thought she might be bipolar. We told her that was nonsense but that she could certainly go talk to one since we knew she was having trouble in school and could obviously use someone else's viewpoint on how she was handling her life.

She went once a week to a woman psychologist in Tucson. In mid-February, Kelly called us and said the counselor wanted to talk to her and to us in a group session. Immediately we knew this discussion would be about drugs. So, on February 11th, a Friday afternoon at 4 o'clock, we met her at the therapist's office. Kelly presented us with a parking ticket she had found on her car for parking on the wrong side of the street. Then we all went inside. In the waiting room was a girl maybe two years older than Kelly. I remember wondering what was wrong with her at that age to have to be seeing a psychologist and thinking that it was sad.

When the counselor called us in, she said, "Kelly has something to tell you. Go ahead, Kelly."

"I'm a drug addict." That was it. I had never expected to hear it like that! "Drug addict." Not "I've been messing around with drugs and want to get serious with my school work and need a little guidance." Noooo…she went all the way to "drug addict." Through my mind went all the stereotypical images: drug addicts, pills, needles, park benches, the movie "Traffic" with Michael Douglas, etc.

Then the counselor asked where we stood and what we wanted to do to help Kelly. We said, "Whatever it

Chapter 6

takes." We never wavered from that pledge. The counselor said since Kelly had good support from her family, her chances were pretty good. This was another new tidbit for me to digest in the following months. I thought, "What exactly did the counselor mean by that? What's this 'chance' business? Here we are; we know now that Kelly has a problem and we'll fix it. What does chance have to do with it?" I was equally pissed off about the tongue ring, which made the counselor incredulous. She said, "Forget the tongue ring—your daughter is a drug addict!" That is how seriously uninitiated I was at recognizing how deep the trouble was that we were in.

The counselor said Kelly should not go back to her room at Yeem's house. We were to take her right from her office straight to an emergency clinic and get a blood test, and then to a psychiatric clinic for detox in the morning. (Later we learned that this is standard procedure on an intervention. You don't want to give the addict a chance to reconsider once she has taken this huge scary step.) The situation was hitting me as serious when the doctors got involved. We had always been good at taking charge and getting things done right. If this was the recommended course, then we were going to do it.

We took Kelly to Yeem's house long enough for her to pack a bag. Then we drove to a hospital in the northwestern part of Tucson. We waited for hours in the emergency room because, obviously, blood tests are way down on the triage list. As we waited, Kelly's boyfriend, Devin, showed up with a basket of items Kelly had apparently phoned him to bring. The two of them sat snuggling together in chairs across from us and I had sad thoughts. "How did it get to this? Why are these two young people in here when everyone else who is in love is out in a restaurant or walking together?" For the next seven years that question would pay me daily and nightly visits. "How did it come to this?"

Finally, it was 10:30 PM. We couldn't wait any longer because we still had a two-hour drive home and an early wake-up to head right back up to Tucson the next day, so we walked out of the emergency waiting room and drove home. The next morning, we did all our horse chores in the wee hours and were at a psychiatric clinic near the same hospital by 8:30 AM.

The psychiatric clinic was our next brand new surreal experience since Kelly's "drug addict declaration" only sixteen hours earlier. I had never been in a psychiatric clinic before. It was a whole new experience: the bathroom had no mirrors—just a metal plate—and Kelly had to remove all of her jewelry when she was accepted inside. After an hour or so, we were called back to talk to the staff. The psychiatrist said that, unfortunately, he saw a lot of young people from our area and knew there was a big drug problem there. He said Kelly should go to rehab. So we went to their office and Kelly proceeded to embarrass me by putting her sandals up on their ottoman and not behaving politely like we taught her to do. (Looking back, now, with a better sense of how Kelly behaved when she was loaded, I realize she was definitely on something then.)

We asked the staff which rehab they recommended. After all, this was not something we had any time to research; we knew absolutely nothing about rehab and we had our daughter packed up and ready to go to one that day. The staff said there was a big price range. Tucson had a really nice one, but it was very expensive and offered amenities like massage, swimming pool, horse therapy

Chapter 6

and sometimes had celebrities. We said, "Kelly doesn't need a massage and she already has a horse she doesn't ride—she just needs the standard service so she can get past this whole thing and back in school." (We were so naïve at the time; we seriously viewed rehab as a treatment you pay for, your kid goes through it, and then you slap your hands together and declare "that's it—all done.")

We ended up selecting one that they said seemed to have a good success rate and was average in price—about $13,000 for 30 days. It was located in Chandler, Arizona, and called "Valley Hope." I thought the name was corny and gave it no more thought. Honestly, it took two more years for me to realize the significance of that name.

CHAPTER 7
Valley Hope

We arrived in Chandler by early afternoon and had our first experience with a rehab clinic. Valley Hope was located right in the Chandler downtown area. It was an older apartment complex which had been converted into the clinic. In fact, you wouldn't actually have known it was a clinic from first look. At that point, Doug and I were in shock mode. Even Kelly, who was high, appeared to be spooked. A staffer met us and gave us a short tour of the lounge, desk area—where the urine testing was located—and the game room. The people milling about were older than Kelly and several of them looked like they had led pretty rough lives. The patients resided in the apartment complex. There was no fence around the clinic and no rules against leaving or having cell phones. Had we even had a little experience in this brave new world, we would never have put Kelly in this clinic. An open clinic like that is for mature people who actually want to be there—maybe even people who have scratched up their last dime and their family's last dime to give them this opportunity. It was not for a person like Kelly, who had no respect for her family's finances and no self-restraint to work at a program with such an open setting.

Kelly wanted us to bring her car to her and we said, "No." We told her she wouldn't need it, but we would bring her bicycle. Then the staff summoned a girl close to Kelly's age to talk to her about what it is like in Valley Hope. Perhaps they sensed we were ready to bolt. While the girls were talking, Doug and I sat outside on a picnic bench and cried—both of us. *How did we get here in just 24 hours? How could we actually drive away and leave our beautiful 18 year-old daughter in the middle of a downtown in an apartment complex filled with drug addicts? What other choice would we have at that time of day since we didn't even know where else we could take her? This place would take all our cash savings.* We couldn't go for the movie star place. We had to try this; the doctors said she should be in a rehab. So when Kelly came out of her session with the girl saying she would be willing to try it, we hugged her good-bye—all of us crying—and drove home for the most solemn four-hour car trip of our lives. What had we just done?

Doug and I (and, one time, Kelly's grandmother) drove up to see Kelly on the weekends. The first weekend she seemed okay. She told us that on the first morning when everyone met in the main gathering room, someone handed her a cup of coffee and a cigarette and said, "Welcome to your new addictions." We were shocked. She needed two more addictions like she needed a hole in the head. Sure enough, she became a heavy smoker and a strong coffee drinker for the rest of her short life. (Kelly never did only a little of anything.)

Chapter 7

On the second weekend, Kelly was not acting right. She was in rehab, so at least we KNEW she wasn't taking drugs otherwise we would have been really worried. She asked us if we could take her to a craft store to buy some beads. Here was an 18 year-old college student acting like she was six years old. On our drive home, we worried together that Kelly's brain might be gone.

The third week was called "Family Week" and the staff encouraged Doug and me both to participate for all five days. However, I drove up to Chandler to attend alone. Doug didn't want to take the time off of work for something he thought I could surely "check the block for." One family member should do it—two seemed like over-kill. We didn't really understand the importance of Family Week. I booked a motel room and, on Monday morning, was given the facilities tour with the other family members. There was a room with shelves of coffee cups all over the walls. They told us the patients decorated their cups and placed them on a shelf. In a year, if the patient stayed sober, he could come back and take his cup with him. I couldn't believe all the cups on the walls! I remember thinking that nobody with a life would bother coming back to a rehab just to get his coffee cup. I was sure that must have been why there were so many left on the walls.

Then came the session where a counselor talked to the families. We sat on chairs in a circle, which I already didn't like. It seemed so "Bob Newhart." The counselor was a lady in her sixties who told us she was a recovering alcoholic and she had two drug-addicted sons on the streets as she spoke. My mouth probably dropped open. *Why would I sit there and take lessons from some woman who obviously royally screwed-up her own life?* I was expecting some doctor, or at least an educated counselor, to give us sound advice on what to do. Instead this woman was telling us how she never gave money to her sons when they came home, but would always feed them a sandwich. *What??? Why, this was so low-life!* Then we learned why everyone was there. Each family member had to introduce himself and give his story. A well-dressed woman about my age said her daughter had been a drug addict ever since she was molested. They had put her in the expensive rehab in Tucson but it didn't help, so now they were trying this one. I thought, *Can you imagine doing this twice??? And did she say the expensive one didn't work??? Her poor daughter must really be screwed-up.*

The people I most remember were this older couple who were plainly dressed and quiet. They sat with their son-in-law, a guy with a mullet. They said their daughter was a teacher but alcohol was messing up her life to the point she did some kind of physical damage to the husband. They said they had been trying to help their daughter for 25 years and they coped by retreating to a cabin in the White Mountains in Arizona. *"Wow,"* I thought. *Their daughter already has her college education and is nice-looking and she has a husband with a mullet and even he is unable to live with her!* I was getting an education, but not comprehending the lessons yet.

We paused for lunch and Kelly left me sitting awkwardly alone in the cafeteria. I thought, "She treats me like crap yet here I was subjecting myself to all this for her sake." At 1:00 PM all the families were to meet in some big room. I was singled out to go to Kelly's counselor's office. "Oh, I'm probably first up for the one-on-one counseling they most likely have planned," I thought. When the counselor met me, she said Kelly was being

Chapter 7

kicked out. Kelly had had two friends delivering drugs to her and she was to leave within 15 minutes because they had zero tolerance for this kind of thing—it poisoned the atmosphere.

I didn't see that coming. My thoughts were coming too fast: "What do I do? Where do I take Kelly? I can't have her at home taking drugs—we wouldn't be able to control her." The counselor said we could wait thirty days and try Valley Hope again and, in the meantime, we could place Kelly in a kind of halfway house for wayward women in Mesa, another city in the greater Phoenix area. It was called "Alice's Wonderland" and was located in the downtown Mesa area.

I helped Kelly scoop all her belongings quickly out of her room and stopped twice for directions to Alice's Wonderland. It was an old small house, literally in the shadows of the skyscrapers. The lady who ran it said she had an available bed and it would be $250 for a week, cash in advance. Again I couldn't believe what I was doing while I was doing it. I was dropping off my 18 year-old daughter in an "Alice's Wonderland" house and driving four hours away. I should have brought her back home, but the course of events had me confused and scared. I was supposed to put a drug addict where the counselors recommended. I called Doug on my cell phone, but he was busy in his office and clearly didn't understand what was happening since he had to compute it all in one ten-minute phone call. I left Kelly in that creepy house and drove home crying all the way.

That evening, Yeem called us to say that Kelly was not staying at Alice's Wonderland and that her boyfriend, Devin, was en route to get her. As I remember the cascade of events, Doug called Devin and asked him not to do it.

DEVIL'S AVATAR

Devin told Doug that Doug couldn't stop him. Doug said to Devin that since he lived in Tucson, he already had an hour and a half head start over us and that Devin clearly had won this round. It was not only bad enough that our daughter was in Alice's Wonderland, but now Doug was having a crude fight with her boyfriend. We were slipping into something, and I knew it was going to be an ugly slide.

CHAPTER 8
Sierra Tucson

That night, Doug and I talked about what we were going to do. There was no way we could wait thirty days and put Kelly right back in the same rehab that wasn't going to help her. She couldn't have an open rehab. We decided there was no point just finding another one similar to Valley Hope. "Let's go to the top," we said, "and get the expensive one. That way we had given her the best there is and if she still isn't helped, at least we know we don't have to search for another one."

We called Sierra Tucson and learned that they had a bed available but it would cost $33,000 for thirty days and they would only take cash (or high-end insurance policies, which we obviously didn't have). We borrowed the money from my mom, since we had just spent $13,000 at Valley Hope for two weeks of nothing or—at best—a lesson. It would be a lot of money to owe my mom, but it would be worth every penny when Kelly walked out in thirty days and went back to school, putting an end to the stupid drug experimentation phase of her life. For

$33,000, it was a foregone successful conclusion as we saw it. $33,000, thirty days, and we would have bought our old Kelly back. Six days later, we had her in the "celebrity clinic."

Compared to Valley Hope, Sierra Tucson was very upscale. The place wouldn't let anyone who was not pre-approved near the patients, ensuring that her friends were not going to be able to bring drugs to her there. Everyone who came had to sign a form saying you would not talk about anyone inside in order to protect the patients' privacy. Smoking was discouraged, and the cafeteria served healthy food. When a patient first arrived, he was placed for three days in a medical clinic for a general health exam and detox if necessary. Kelly needed a health checkup. She needed a sanctuary that would get her out of the storm in order for her to have a chance to think clearly without the influence of substances. She needed time out from chaos.

One of the first things they did in Sierra Tucson was to test Kelly for ADD. Although Kelly did tell us about this—and said she tested off the chart for almost every determiner—we never saw the paperwork at the time because she was over 18 years old.

Here is another tip: Once your kid hits eighteen, you don't get access to any medical or rehab information even though you are paying for everything—unless she lets you. Unfortunately I only read her test results seven years later from her files after she died. We didn't realize she was given her test results on paper; otherwise we would have asked her to let us see them. With Kelly, you needed to know what questions to ask otherwise nothing was volunteered. On the ADD graph I could see the line for narcissism went off the chart. Handwritten in the mar-

Chapter 8

gin by someone were the words "inflated sense of ego (inside there is insecurity), opinionated, cocky attitude, center of attention, entitled to special treatment, arrogance about drugs." Another line off the chart was Risk Taking Behavior defined for her in the margin as "dangerous risk taking, impulsive, quick-fix, illegal behavior, breaking the rules—/rebellious behavior." The Illegal Drugs graph line went off the page followed closely by Alcohol, explained in Kelly's case by "addiction, addictive behavior, quick-fix/immediate gratification." Other graph lines that were high reflect fear of abandonment, unstable moods—unstable relationships, black and white thinking, impulsiveness, self-questioning. Finally, there were the lines indicating self-defeating behavior/sabotaging, low self-esteem/guilt, being your own worst enemy and undermining self.

We paid extra for an MRI scan, because we were afraid Kelly might have damaged her brain. Since we knew about this procedure, we asked for the results several times and only had a vague answer from Kelly's psychologist at the very end revealing that it turned out okay. We weren't prepared for the privacy clause and should have been more aggressive about finding out from Kelly exactly what she learned. Of course, she would have construed that as prying and probably wouldn't have told us anything.

But at least we knew Kelly had a condition, ADD, and we had a place to start trying to help—a toehold. We could research ADD and maybe figure out what could be done. We bought some books on the subject and went on the internet. Right off the bat I realized my mother had ADD and nobody knew it! She had baskets with papers all over her house yet could never find a receipt or document. All my life she has backed the car over suitcases and grocery bags, lost her jewelry in ditzy ways, missed appointments or arrived for them a day or two early, etc. I never thought anything of it because that was just how my mother has always been. No wonder I never recognized ADD in Kelly. My mother's case was different from Kelly's in that she had common sense and a survival instinct which has enabled her to live a long life, overcoming obstacles despite no medication or substance abuse.

Again, as when Kelly was at the last rehab, we drove up to visit Kelly on the first two weekends. Her grandmother came along and Yeem visited her. During one visit I asked Kelly why she couldn't just enjoy a beautiful sunset and let that provide her a natural "high" as it does for most people. Her answer was telling. She said, "Because I would only think how much better it would be on drugs." *Could this kind of thinking be fixed? Would this place do it?*

There was another disquieting thing she told me on one of those weekend visits. She said she was completely aware of how bad and wrong it was to try drugs, but there wasn't anything Doug and I could have done to stop her—curiosity about them compelled her. But, on the other hand, she also knew that she had a safety net if she ever reached a point where it got too scary or serious: us. She told me she knew we would always be there to rescue her, although she would have to do the "hard part" of telling us.

So, that was Kelly's escape plan: rely on parents to end the party, send all the kids home and put her to bed! Lacking self-control, she had been relying on us to provide external control. And, sure enough, there we were still trying our hardest to provide it—except now we had to hire professionals. Sierra Tucson had to fix everything

Chapter 8

this time, because we knew nothing about drug abuse and addiction.

Family Week

Doug and I both came for Family Week this time (no way was I going to go through that alone again). It wasn't easy because we had to wake up at 4 AM to feed the horses and clean the stalls and then drive two hours to Tucson each morning. The days in Family Week were grueling in that so much information was coming at us like it was being shot out of a fire hose. We got blasted with our new frightening reality. At the end of each day we drove back and took care of the animals for the evening and fell into bed for sleepless nights digesting all we had learned in the day. Kelly thanked us for going through all of that for her which reminded us how nice she had been in the good old days before drugs.

The first thing the counselors told us when they introduced themselves was that most of them were recovering drug addicts and alcoholics. They understood patients and their family dynamics in ways that would be almost impossible for someone who hadn't been through the experience intimately to understand. (This certainly explained the recovering alcoholic lady counselor with the two drug addict sons from the first rehab.)

Too bad you aren't issued a manual when you get thrown into this new alternate world of drug addiction. There are things that make sense but that you can't see because you are looking at everything through a lens that never needed an adjustment for this new setting.

We were finally going to get a peek at what went on in a rehab. We definitely were offered a wealth of knowledge even though at least half of it only really registered with us much later.

Here is what I remember about Family Week:

The family members were put into groups of about ten, covering a broad spectrum of Americans. In our group, there was a young person whose father was an alcoholic. This poor girl was agonizing over saving her dad, who clearly didn't want rescuing. It was painful to watch her crying and trying so hard. There was a woman who was attending for her son but she, herself, had already been through Sierra Tucson. She claimed Sierra Tucson was her "birth" place. She was such a warm and sincere person that we didn't doubt she believed it. Doug and I thought that it was sad to think of a rehab as your birthplace. There was a well-to-do older couple whom we dubbed "Lovey and Thurston" (as in "Howell the III"). You got the impression "Thurston" had never worked a day in his life for money. They were there for their daughter's addiction and talked about some effect this had on one of their vacation houses or the redecoration thereof. Their situation was a little hard to relate to, but I'm sure in their world these problems were as monumental to them as ours were to us.

Another person I recall clearly was a no-nonsense CEO who was about our age and was there for his son. We felt most comfortable around him because he didn't like the hand-holding circle, the hugging, and the "Serenity Prayer" reciting any more than we did. The Serenity Prayer is THE major prayer recited in rehab:

Chapter 8

"God grant me the serenity to accept the things I cannot change, courage to change the things I can, and wisdom to know the difference."

In fact, Doug and I purposely situated ourselves so that we could just read the prayer off of the two framed copies of it on just about any wall in Sierra Tucson. Once the week was over, we wouldn't need to say it anymore—our kid would be all cured—so why would we bother memorizing it? We just wanted to "get 'er done" and get our kid out of there and move on from that unfortunate blip in our lives.

The first lecture we went to was a cold "just the facts, ma'am" straight-up information dump on the medical realities of addictions so that we could have an informed understanding of the physical and chemical changes which occur in the body and brain. We definitely started paying attention and we were starting to get scared. Afterward, we asked a counselor what percentage of people really make it and recover. He answered dead-pan seriously that nobody knows for sure, but the full recovery rate is probably around twenty percent. Even with that statistic, we were sure Kelly was going to be in that number. Not even a little doubt did we have.

Then we asked about all the therapies offered at Sierra Tucson, such as art therapy, equine therapy, hypnotism, acupuncture, massage, etc. We asked which ones worked the best. He responded that, honestly, the only thing that has ever worked has been the Twelve-Step Program. They had already explained that to us and had given a short history of the founders, Bill Wilson and Dr. Bob Smith, in an earlier lecture. Apparently Bill, an alcoholic on the brink of death, had a miraculous spiritual experience and stopped drinking. Afterward, he and his friend, Dr. Bob, went on to create the Twelve-Step Program, divinely inspired by his supernatural recovery. All Doug and I heard was the word "miracle" and we were instantly turned-off. We wanted REAL tangible help for Kelly, not something we didn't believe in and couldn't understand (at least not at that time).

Overall, the Twelve-Step Program didn't seem applicable to Kelly. For one thing, it sounded like a lot of work and effort—which she avoided like the plague. Also, Kelly surely wouldn't like the religiousness of the program. But, even after hearing this bit of bad news, we were still absolutely certain—no doubt in our minds—that Kelly would be in that twenty percent who succeeded. This was just one tool she most likely wouldn't use, but it didn't sound like a big deal at the time.

One of the big messages Sierra Tucson was trying to impart to the family members was the need for us to protect ourselves. They had training sessions on what they called "boundaries." If the addicted family member was dragging the rest of the family down, you have to draw a line in the sand beyond which you wouldn't go in order to save yourself from being destroyed as well. I remember telling the group that I pledged to do whatever it took to get Kelly off of drugs and that I was prepared to keep that pledge. The counselor asked me if I would still charge on, even if Kelly didn't want off of drugs. I told her I would NEVER stop. She kept asking me, "But what if she doesn't want help? What if she doesn't want to stop?" This exchange went on until the counselor decided it was no use. Looking back, the funny thing about it was how clearly I could see that the girl in our group who wouldn't stop trying to save her father was expending a lot of emo-

Chapter 8

tional capital in a fight she would not win. But I was sure my case was different. Kelly was at stake here.

There was another lesson I learned in our group. I told the members that this drug stuff was embarrassing to me because I have some friends who don't understand what we're going through and they are distancing themselves from Doug and me. I am sure a lot of acquaintances of ours who learned our daughter had a drug problem probably thought we were bad parents. I know I would probably have had those thoughts myself. So concerned was I about our standing with the people of our small community, that I mentioned this worry to several counselors. One just said plainly, "then you need new friends because the ones you have aren't real ones." This was going to take some digesting—the thought that my successful drug-free friends were the problem and not Kelly's drug addiction. This would mean a complete shift in the way I processed my thoughts. Another counselor just looked at me with incomprehension. He said he would rather be with people who were drug addicts or alcoholics any day because they have been through life's wringer and are much more compassionate, nonjudgmental, and overall nicer people. Here was yet another new concept: drug addicts and alcoholics as actually being preferable as friends. I would come to see how right he was in the near future and his lesson gave me the fortitude to make some friend changes.

Once, when Doug and I were sitting in a lobby with some other people waiting for a session or lecture to start, an older care-worn man came in to "chat" with us. He just started talking about his life-long battle with alcoholism and how he struggled every day to stay sober and just plodded on baby step by baby step, day by day, happy to just win another day substance-free. His name was Gus and when he started talking, we thought "Oh, brother, we're a captive audience in here and we're going to have to listen to this guy ramble on." Yes, he did tell his story in a rambling way with a slow pace, but it was the evenly plodding beat that really made his story fascinating to us. Here was a man who should have been worn out in his battle to stay sober each day but only through a Herculean human effort forged on to encounter the same enemy the next day. Day after day after day. Plod. Plod. Plod. You could feel the sheer effort it took him to be able to arrive sober at Sierra Tucson and tell his story.

On our drive home that night, we talked about Gus. The dim light of a horrible new concept was just beginning to dawn on us: this drug problem Kelly had might have been bigger than we realized. Those people at Sierra Tucson were telling us something but we weren't really hearing it. The "just the facts" drug doctor, the lady who was "born" there, the need to change friends, family members protecting themselves, the point-blank counselor with the twenty percent survivor statement. They were all telling us in bits and pieces that what we were up against was huge—virtually insurmountable without monumental effort by the addict and even then with the grace of God. And then there was Gus himself—the embodiment of that struggle. How many people could actually be like Gus and put out that kind of effort? He was weaving together, with his story, everything we had been told so far about the pain and challenge of surviving addictions. He wasn't really a counselor, just a guy who "got it."

During the whole family week we were able to eat lunch with Kelly and sit in on the some of the same lectures together. We noticed Kelly was not participating with her group or paying attention to the lectures. She was always

Chapter 8

just writing in her journal. For $1,000 a day, I wished she would have been more engaged, but what could we have done? You could never make Kelly do anything.

On Friday, the last day of Family Week, we were finally going to be allowed to go to Kelly's counseling group and talk to her with the mediation of her counselor. Up until that point, the families were kept separated from the counseling group. It was Doug's and my turn to meet them for the first time while the other members of Kelly's group were allowed to listen to our family spill our worries and hash out our problems. This was going to be the big revelation. Secretly, I suppose Doug may have been wondering if there was something that had happened between me and Kelly that caused her to turn to drugs. I know I was secretly wondering the reverse—if she and he had some big issue.

Lo and behold, the moment of revelation arrived and Kelly produced some infantile drawing of her as the sun with Doug, my mom, and me as the orbiting planets. Her "problem" was that we were overly involved with her life and wouldn't leave her alone enough to be free. She resented us for putting her in summer camp when she was ten and for making her do the SAT class. She resented Doug for helping her too much with paperwork relating to her summer job (tax forms) and her college application. She resented me for being critical of her diet and for calling her fat (which I never did, although I said she would get fat if she kept eating potato chips as a vegetarian diet). The counselor immediately took Kelly's side and basically told us some quote about how we didn't have a life of our own and lived through her.

We couldn't believe it! She got here because we weren't breathing down her throat and we allowed her too much freedom with her car and didn't snoop in her room. She abused her freedom and her naïve parents and took drugs. Doug and I walked outside stunned. Then, suddenly, he became visibly upset and told me to wait a minute. He ran back inside and spoke to Kelly's counselor in the hall. I could hear him asking her, "You mean, that's IT? My daughter is here and that's the reason?"

It's just as well family week ended for us right after that final revelation. After that we couldn't take any more. On the thirtieth day of rehab we went to Sierra Tucson to get Kelly. She had a session with some counselors during that last week concerning her continued recovery after she left Sierra Tucson. They recommended a "sober living" house (I use this term interchangeably with half-way house) situation for at least three months—longer would be even better. In a sober living house, Kelly would be supervised, urine-tested, and counseled, and would have to obey a curfew, but would still be afforded enough freedom to go to school or get a job. We had no say in this, and she had already told them she would not go to a half-way house. She was going back to Yeem's and back to school, even though they told her that was a bad idea. If we knew all the things we do now, we would never have gone along with her plan. At the time, we were not financially flush. We still owed my mom and had no idea how dangerous the time was right after rehab. We wanted to believe Kelly was fine now and was simply going back to school.

CHAPTER 9
After Rehabs·

In the first week after she was out of Sierra Tucson, I went with Kelly to the University of Arizona to help her withdraw from her classes without incurring an academic penalty. We still had to pay the tuition and took a loss on the text books. Doug had to fly back to Vermont to be with his mother in her final days as she was dying from cancer, so he was unable to go with us. Doug had barely returned, at the end of Kelly's second week out of rehab, when we received a panicked call from Kelly's roommate Yeem telling us that Kelly had packed up her Volkswagen and was getting ready to drive to Los Angeles by herself. Our vulnerable eighteen-year-old was heading to California alone! We were an hour and a half away; we were helpless.

At least Kelly called us from the road. She said she was relapsing because she was seeing her same friends who were all still doing the old bad things. One of the guys from her Sierra Tucson group told her she could stay at his place in Los Angeles which he shared with another man and go to Alcoholics Anonymous meetings there where a huge community of recovering drug addicts and alcoholics live. She said she was scared but she HAD to do this; she had to get out of Tucson in order to save herself.

This did not sound good at all: an eighteen-year-old staying with a recovering drug addict and another guy in L.A. We asked her not to do it, but asking never worked with Kelly. She wouldn't tell us where she was going. A couple of weeks later, Kelly called saying she had to get out of that situation and ended up leaving her computer at the guy's house. Some other people in the AA group she was attending were helping her find a half-way house. She had a meeting with Zena, the lady who ran a sober living house called Herbert House in Santa Monica, and was told she could go there. We kept telling her to make sure to get her computer back before it was too late, but she gave some story about how she couldn't because the guy wasn't home or didn't answer her calls. All that time we were angry about how careless Kelly was with our resources.

It was six years later when Kelly told us that she had been raped. Only recently did I read in her files what happened.

Resentments against David Letocks (from Kelly's files):

> *1) Having ulterior motives in convincing me to come to L.A. to get sober.*
> *FEAR: - not getting to get fare to L.A.—safely from Tucson*
>   *- David's disapproval*

Chapter 9

> *SELF-SEEKING: - I wanted everything he offered me and was willing to pay a price.*
> *- I knew there was some form of payback and just went with it.*
> *DISHONESTY: I went along with it despite my instincts.*
>
> *2) Slyly coercing me into his bed[room]*
> *FEAR: - getting stuck in the sexual situation I ended up in.*
> *SELF-SEEKING: - I wanted his stuff and I didn't expect my suck-up efforts to result poorly.*
> *- I didn't want to lose his offerings or go against him.*
> *DISHONEST: - I acted as though I had no idea what was really going on.*
>
> *3) Having sex with me to keep me in the compromising position of being completely dependent on him through sex.*
> *FEAR: - being a prostitute and codependent on him.*
> *- saying no and being in an awkward situation*
> *- Falling into that trap.*
> *SELF-SEEKING: I expect to have control of a situation if I put out the sex. In this I lost control, my whole set-up and security in L.A.*
> *DISHONESTY: - I told him I was more into it than I was.*
> *- I didn't tell anyone and avoided dealing with the situation until it became unmanageable.*

(By the way, I have changed all names used in my book except for Kelly's, Doug's, and mine. Initially, I was going to leave the real name of the pig who raped Kelly so he could be publicly shamed. However, prudence (i.e.

fear of lawyers) has prevailed and I have decided to leave it to God to pass out punishment.)

We said we would pay for Kelly's rent at the sober living house and for a psychologist and psychiatrist. The psychologist would be the one to help guide her out of whatever was going wrong in her life and the psychiatrist was needed so someone could continue to prescribe the prescriptions she had been put on for ADD in Sierra Tucson. I remember wondering when we had to pay for all this help, why she couldn't just listen to her parents. We would guide her for free if she would just let us. She really liked her psychologist, Dr. Jay, whom she met at an AA meeting. He was very experienced with recovery and took Kelly on as his patient. We were very lucky she found him, too, because he gave us a break on his "real" rates recognizing we weren't wealthy. Kelly was very happy to be Dr. Jay's patient and seemed to actually have a relationship with him built on truth. We certainly didn't have that going for us with Kelly. Her psychiatrist was an older man who was still "into" Freud. She thought having a Freudian psychiatrist was cool, but we didn't think she was helped by that.

She moved into Herbert House in June, 2004, and said she really liked it. She went to AA meetings and met a lot of friends who were trying hard to stay sober, one of whom was a man close to our age, Tony. He was one of those people who "got it" and was trying to help the community and doing the hard work of keeping himself away from others who would drag him back down. We were happy Kelly had found such a good friend whom she admired and who was looking out after her while being a good influence. Tony called Doug and me many times through the next six years to ask about Kelly. She later

Chapter 9

stopped contact with him because he represented an expectation of staying sober that she wouldn't/couldn't meet and because she was afraid that that kind of confrontation would hurt her self-esteem.

At her AA meetings, Kelly found a sponsor who helped her work the Twelve-Step Program. Looking back, the Herbert House experience was the closest Kelly came to working her way to sobriety. I have found at least four notebooks filled with soul-searches and amends she set to paper, whether she actually told them to the intended recipients yet or not. There was even a list of stores someday she hoped to repay for petty theft and she wrote of a guilty conscience for having compulsively taken forks from every restaurant in which she had a meal. Some of her other amends I have already transcribed earlier in this book, but here is one for her grandmother:

> *Oma* (German word for grandmother)
> *Abusing her money, trust, car, gifts*
> *Lying to her the way I lied to Mom and Dad*
> *Not acknowledging her $$$ for treatment—wasting treatment*
> *Visiting her, stopping by for gifts, holidays, dinners, her friends (etc.) high & lying*
> *Avoiding her*
> *Not taking her into account when I moved; left treatment, etc.*
> *Stealing her meds, money & stuff*

For Kelly, we could tell she put out a tremendous effort to try to climb out of the ditch she was in. She went through much of the work to recover, but was foiled by her inability to trust in her higher power. I accept blame for this. Although we were a moral family, we were not religious in the sense that we didn't belong to a certain denomination. Actually, when Kelly was three years old, I realized I should be doing something about her religious upbringing and I tried to go back to my roots by rejoining the Catholic Church. I had to go through a remedial course and then Kelly was baptized. I went to church with Kelly for two years and could do no more. I simply didn't believe and there was no way I could fake it for the next fifteen years. We told Kelly that there was a God, but we didn't believe any specific denomination was the only true way to worship. I told her nature was my church. I realize, now that this may have been a mistake because years later when she needed that faith, she was unable to grab onto it. Even though I am looking at a notebook now that is filled with her attempts, I see that she couldn't get past the second and third steps of the Twelve-Step Program, the ones pertaining to accepting a higher power,. I told one counselor in Sierra Tucson my guilty feelings about this and she said, "You did the best you could AT THE TIME." That phrase has stuck with me because it is so forgiving when you are measuring everything using harsh hindsight.

Kelly did leave a poignant letter to her Drug Addiction in her Twelve-Step workbook:

> *Dear Drug Addiction,*
> *You have been a major part of my life for the last three years, but I am eliminating you and all of your baggage so that I can move on and save myself. Please take it personally, you are a vile bitch.*
> *I will miss all of the parties we spent together. I will miss the temporary euphoria and the way you make me feel warm and fuzzy inside. I will miss how I could reach you at four or five different phone num-*

Chapter 9

> *bers. I will miss your pretty colors. I will miss the way you make music sound and the way you make walls wiggle. I will miss hanging out. I will miss eating junk food with you. I will miss meeting other people that are automatically my friends because we all know you. I will miss having an escape route from reality through you.*
>
> *I will not miss your incriminating smell. I will not miss the holes you burn in my brain and the way you slow me down and pull me down. I will not miss your lies. I will not miss the aftershock you leave every time I come down and you fade away. I will not miss wasting money so we can have more time to hang out. I will not miss the lies you make me tell. I will not miss your fan club. I will not miss your grasp on me.*
>
> *I am angry that you soiled my morality. I am angry that you made my grades fall and my attendance slip. I am angry that you have all of my memories in your haze. I am angry that you made my parents afraid of me—you made them lose all trust and faith in me. I am angry that you deceived me. You manipulated my brain and told me that you could help me. I am angry that you ate all of my money and my parents' money. I am angry that you made my friends separate from me. I am angry that you killed my brain cells and stole my motivation. I am angry that you fucked with my body, you made me sick, you made me lazy. You made me lose a lot of sleep and time. I am angry that you intervened in every important part of my life.*
>
> *I am sorry for believing you. I am sorry for giving you everything under blind faith.*
>
> *I do not appreciate you. I have no respect for you and I do not need you!*

Things seemed to be going well for a while. In September (three months after she arrived at Herbert

House), Kelly's wisdom teeth needed to be removed, which meant the Herbert House team had to supervise her visit and her medications. The next week, Doug's family in Vermont was holding a memorial for his mother. Kelly wanted to attend and we were not going to deny her that. We sent her a ticket and met up with her in the Dallas airport. We all went on together to Vermont. The whole visit quickly became a disaster when Kelly began complaining about severe pain from her wisdom teeth extractions. Finally we took her to a dentist who gave her some pain killers. We didn't think about taking the medication away from her like a baby and, sure enough, she helped herself to all of it in one whack. The memorial and the dinner were ruined for us and the relatives got a first-hand look at what we were going through.

Before we left, Kelly wanted to attend an AA meeting held in a church basement in downtown Brattleboro. While she was there, Doug and I took a walk around the town. It was filled with young people just hanging around the streets. A lot of them were begging us for money. We actually gave one hard-looking young woman some, which we ordinarily would not have done but, at the time, all we could think was that Kelly could be her someday if Kelly didn't straighten out. I remember feeling that new sensation of true empathy for people and how they can just fall into situations. Maybe that woman had worried parents somewhere. We were transmogrifying into nicer people through our ordeal.

When Kelly got back to Herbert House and told them what had happened with the dental medication, they had to decide whether or not she should be allowed to stay. They decided to allow her because she was out of their control and her parents weren't smart enough to keep bet-

Chapter 9

ter tabs on her. Things began going downhill for Kelly after that relapse. She had been amassing parking tickets, which she just put in a drawer—"out of sight, out of mind." When the tickets were overdue and doubled in penalty, we would receive them at our home address because, ultimately, the car was registered to us. There were over $2,000 worth of them.

Kelly met another Herbert House resident, a woman older than her by twelve years or more, who was kicked out in short order for shoplifting, but not before she imparted the advanced skills of her craft to Kelly. On the phone, Kelly told us all about her new friend, who was "so cool...so much fun," etc. The magic of trying hard for sobriety became a farce. In November, Herbert House helped Kelly get a job on the Santa Monica Pier in a gift shop. Although the idea was good, in hindsight this was also bad because Kelly was out in a highly drug-trafficked area with no supervision. I automatically assumed she was sneaking drugs because our relationship with her was deteriorating once again. Now we were just hearing about how much fun she was having (which we had learned was never a good sign with Kelly). I found out later that I was wrong, though, because I found a post mortem notebook all about her stay in Herbert House and read that she was proud of herself for resisting temptation until one day in December.

That fateful December day must have been around the same time I called the Herbert House because Kelly wasn't answering her cell phone. Zena, the lady who ran it, asked if Kelly had "told me." I asked, "Told me what?" Zena explained that Kelly had been kicked out a few days earlier. Apparently she and a friend were doing "whippits" in the kitchen (sniffing the pressurizing gas that comes out of a spray whipped cream can). Zena said this was grounds for expulsion even if it didn't seem to be a hard drug, because if someone was doing this, they were not serious about recovery. We were very sorry for this turn of events because we knew Kelly really liked it at the Herbert House and we felt she was in a safe place while she was there.

We were worried about where Kelly was. She called us, finally—after her money ran out and she couldn't stay in cheap motels any longer. She told us she was pondering the option of living out of her car. Her employer told her she could do that and shower under or near the pier. We couldn't understand how Kelly could even contemplate that. And what kind of person would make a suggestion like that to someone who couldn't take care of herself?

Kelly drove home right after that and I have one very clear memory of the day she arrived home in her car. She stood in the doorway and told Doug and me that her life was in shambles, she had no future and she might just as well use drugs. She said she had had a "good run," which was a statement that alarmed us. *"A good run?" She was only 19!* I guess for the very first time we were confronted with the thought of Kelly's drug problem being a permanent dilemma for her. Up until then, we were following a path to getting her back on track. But there was no more track to follow. We had to grasp that Kelly had eaten through a lot of her options: two rehabs, a halfway house, and a lost education.

Around this time we invited our old friend and Kelly's confidant "Uncle Markus" over for dinner only to discover the next day that he had brought her a present: some OxyContin and morphine. We couldn't believe it!

Chapter 9

This made no sense coming from someone we trusted so much. We never spoke to him again.

The Devil was bringing out the evil in everyone whom he could touch with his avatar, our daughter.

CHAPTER 10
The Army Idea

Panic started setting in. Kelly had already declared her life directionless and demonstrated how she was counterbalancing that problem—with more drugs. The idea of her going into the military was my natural next option, after all, Doug and I had both served and we really liked it. We had never promoted the option to her before because we wanted her to get her education first. Having tried everything else, the idea of military service was looking like our last hope. In the military, Kelly would have to account for her drug abuse, but we reasoned that lots of kids do that and the military works its magic on them and squares them away. It would offer self-discipline, organization, and structure—all the things we saw as essential for her to climb out of her ditch. Even so, we knew it would be a giant gamble. I told Doug, "This can go either way, but if it goes south, what have we lost from where we stand now?"

Even Kelly realized this was a last opportunity for her and as lacking in military decorum or demeanor as she was, she embraced the idea. She even tried to get her best friend, Miles, to join on the "Buddy System" with her, but he wasn't ready to take such a leap. She went to the Air Force recruiters, first, and was unabashedly upfront with them about her drug abuse. They told her to go across the hall to the Army. Kelly couldn't believe she had been rejected by the military! She had always assumed that she was above that. With her new outlook, she did go across the hall and was accepted by the Army because this time she didn't mention a drug history—and they, luckily, didn't ask. They gave her an aptitude test which she scored well on and they offered her whatever she would like. We told her not to pick language school because they would investigate her background and she'd be kicked out. So she selected "91X, Mental Health Specialist." As crazy as that sounds, she thought she would really be good at the job because she already had so much experience with shrinks and messed-up people. She thought that by helping others she would be helping herself—like in the last step of the Twelve Steps. (I don't know why, but it all seemed to make great sense when we were desperate with no alternatives.)

Kelly actually stayed drug-free for a whole month to pass the urine test. We drove her up to Phoenix to a hotel and she "shipped out" the next day for basic training. Then we waited and hoped and paid off all her debts so that her financial record would be clean. There were thousands of dollars in debts on her credit cards, bank overdrafts, and parking tickets. I think this was the point where I was starting to pray. I hadn't prayed on my knees in a long time and I hoped God would forgive me for starting then when I really, really, *really* needed him.

Chapter 10

Kelly's Army Misadventure

During basic training, Kelly called us and wrote us about her trials and tribulations. I would say she seemed to even like her adventure. The guys were all slobbering over her and the other girls looked up to her as a nineteen-year-old "with a past" and, of course, Kelly was fun. She said the drill sergeants called her names like "Area 51" and "Psychic Hotline." They laughed in disbelief that she enlisted to be a Mental Health Specialist. One drill sergeant made her wear two bras to keep the guys toned down. We found a file labeled "Unrequited Love" after she died filled with love letters from smitten soldiers. She told of her adventures going to church (to get out of duty) and how she survived three months of strenuous exercise eating only peanut butter for protein (since the Army wasn't "vegetarian-friendly"). She said she even had meaningful "human" discussions with her drill sergeant toward the end and that he was actually "cool." The letters were great—Kelly was at her best and off of drugs. I'm sorry I didn't save them.

On the final march of basic training, Kelly broke her hip carrying a rucksack that was just too heavy for her small frame. She was crushed (so to speak) because that evening was the big ceremony out in the field when they gave the graduates their coins. She made it to the end, but didn't make it to "The End." They let her go home to convalesce for a month. This was the worst possible turn of events. She had been drug-free for four months by then and was really stoked about going to her Advanced Individual Training at Fort Sam Houston in San Antonio, Texas. She had convinced herself that she would get recycled and have to do the whole basic training all over again—even though she was told she would not. I don't think Kelly was home one week before she found all of her old "homies" and relapsed.

We realized that, somehow, we had to preoccupy her and pass the three weeks with her at home as quickly and safely as possible. I had the idea of a cruise for three days down the coast from San Diego for a stop in Ensenada, Mexico. After all, if she had to go to Iraq, we would be glad we had the time together. We invited her grandmother and her friend Julie to come along.

Things didn't go well. Kelly mortified her grandmother with her behavior, smoking cigars in her bikini on the deck, gambling in the casino, and being drugged-out and leaving Julie alone most of the time. When the cruise ship docked in Ensenada, Mexico, and let the passengers off for the day, I had another major moment of clarity. Kelly and Julie were off driving rental all-terrain vehicles around Ensenada while my mom, Doug, and I walked around and shopped.

We went into an old church and there was a statue of Jesus near the altar. There were many Mexicans in line for their chance to kneel at this statue and touch Jesus's feet. For the first time, it hit me: This is what it comes to in the end. When you can't do anything more and you have no more means or resources and your options are all gone, then it comes to this: kneeling and rubbing Jesus's feet. We were certainly at that point. The feet of the statue had been rubbed by so many people in the same desperate boat as we were in, for one reason or another, that the paint was long gone and the features were smooth. I didn't get in line, but I understood for the first time how people all have to eventually come to rub the deity's feet. There comes a point when there is nothing else you can do, you

Chapter 10

are powerless—all that is left for you is to hope. That was my first extremely potent introduction to the concept of hope and it explained a lot, including the name of Kelly's first rehab, "Valley Hope." Finally, I "got it!" (Of course, it's also quite a clever play on names. Phoenix is called "The Valley of the Sun," hence: "Valley" Hope.)

After our cruise returned to California, we had left one day open for Kelly to show us her sober living house in L.A., and maybe to find Tony or Dr. Jay and introduce us. Instead, she crashed out in the airport hotel at 4 PM and we ended up taking Julie out for dinner. I remember my mom looking down at Kelly lying in the bed with braids in her hair and remarking how Kelly could still manage to look like an angel when she slept. That summed things up: there were two girls in that body—one angel and one devil. I wondered if sleep was the only time Kelly could catch a break from their incessant conflict with one another. Once, in Sierra Tucson, she told me she really did feel that an angel and a devil were sitting on her shoulders, but the problem was that she would always listen to the wrong one and make bad decisions. *What an easy way to help her, I thought.* I told her to call me anytime that happens and I would tell her which one to obey. She never called me. Then again, "just say 'no'" sounded easy to me, too.

After we got home from the cruise, Kelly only had a few days left to go before she had to get back to basic training at Fort Leonard Wood, Missouri. We planned a "last supper" for her: a vegetarian meal with all kinds of grilled vegetables. Before dinner, Kelly said she was going to town to say good-bye to all her friends and said that if we wanted her to bring anything back with her, we should let her know. That night, Doug and I sat an hour at the table waiting for her and finally we ate without her. All of a sudden both of us looked at each other stricken with horror. *NO!!! She wouldn't do this!!! No! NO! NO!* We ran to her bedroom and sure enough, she had packed all her things, leaving just enough mess for us not to notice.

To Army people like us, the very thought of someone being AWOL (Absent Without Leave) strikes primal terror, calling to mind the idea of life on the lam in Mexico or Canada and never seeing your family again. We were beside ourselves. Our blood pressures skyrocketed and fear kept our adrenaline spiking. *What do we do?* Doug started calling Kelly's friends. Julie was shocked. Then we called Miles. No answer. We called his mom, Lana, who also had been trying to reach him. This made her freak out. She ran to his room and realized that he, most likely, went with Kelly.

We couldn't sleep that night. We called the police to make a missing persons report the next morning, and a policeman came to our house. I was so angry that Kelly would put her parents through this. We were worried sick, wondering if Kelly and Miles were in Mexico or Canada. During that time I began kneeling at our windowsill to pray for Kelly and for us. My mother was so upset about everything she would call every day because she couldn't tell anyone else this junk and had no other outlet for her angst. *Who do you tell these kinds of things to, anyway?* My mom was worried about Doug and me and whether our marriage can hold up through this sort of turmoil. I don't need to be taught lessons twice—I understand the "nothing is for sure" lesson, and I was spooked. As for Doug, a quiet "still waters run deep" kind of guy, I watched him slip outside to cry many times.

Chapter 10

During the third week, there was a break in the case. Miles's mom was notified by her bank that a withdrawal from her son's trust fund was initiated in Orlando, Florida. Apparently, she and Miles had a joint account so one couldn't take out money until 24 hours after the other had been notified. Lana called Doug and they made a plan to get on separate flights that same day and meet up in the Orlando Airport in order to stake out the bank's parking lot the following morning. (It was a crazy plan, but that's how desperate we were.) Unfortunately, Doug and Lana missed them because Miles was able to withdraw the money on the evening before.

After searching all the Twelve-Step meetings and hotels near the bank, Doug flew back home the next day without even staying in a hotel. Lana later told me that Miles and Kelly burned through $20,000 on their spree. Eventually, around the thirtieth day of being AWOL, the Volkswagen self-destructed and the jig was up. They called home, and Miles got a ticket back to Sierra Vista, while Kelly got one back to basic training in Missouri. Miles told his mom he was sorry to put her through the month of worry, but that he, personally, had had the best time of his life.

Kelly showed back up at basic training and didn't get as much as a slap on the wrist. No extra duty was given to her, just a reduction in rank, and they sent her as fast as they could to training in San Antonio—to become someone else's problem. Upon arrival there, she learned that she had missed her class's starting date and would have to wait around three months for the next one to start. This would be boring, which was very bad news. She sneaked off the fort to be with other soldiers who were allowed the privilege (and I'm sure did other bad things I don't even know about). Meanwhile, I got a call from Lana informing me that we were going to be mothers-in-law. *News to me!* Lana and Miles were picking out the rings and he would be taking them (via car trip) to San Antonio that week. I talked to Kelly immediately on the phone and she said something like, "Oh yeah, Miles is going to join the Army and we'll get extra money for being married and between us we'll have the most awesome CD collection! I can see being married for six years." I was disgusted. I asked Kelly how she could treat marriage so lightly when she came from a home where her parents were married 25 years and I asked her not to do it. Please not to do it! She said she wanted a ring and she was going to get married. By that time I realized she must have been on something again—it was drug behavior.

Miles visited Kelly, she took his ring, and he joined the Army to carry out his part of the plan. While he was in basic training, she went AWOL again. This time she took a Greyhound to L.A.—because the bus to Las Vegas had already left; there was no deeper plan to it than that. As soon as she got there, she pawned her new ring for $300.00 and smoked crack with a woman and her husband whom she had traveled with on the bus. When those people started getting violent, she ran away and met up with some Mexican man who took her to his parent's house. Then she and he left to join up with a roving band of drug addicts who sold cleaning products door to door. (No. I'm not making this up.) There was a quota Kelly would have to sell in order to earn some drugs for the evening. The whole vanload of weirdos would stay in a single cheap motel room each night. Kelly told me later that one lady whose door they knocked on said to her, "Don't you

Chapter 10

have parents, honey?" That really stung. I wish I could have told that lady, "YES, Kelly has good parents who would die if they knew she was at your door."

One evening about two weeks after Kelly went AWOL for the second time, her old sober friend, Tony, from her Herbert House days, called us and said Kelly had called him and was in trouble, "She is at a motel in Chandler, Arizona, and you need to get to her as fast as you can." We jumped in our car and drove the four-hour trip in just three. We pulled up to the parking lot of the motel Tony told us to go to along the I-10 highway, and Kelly jumped into the back seat of our car yelling, "Go! Go! Go!" Like in the movies. We sped away and I got a glimpse of the van arriving with some really scary people in it. Kelly was so drugged-out, she lay down in the back seat and told us she liked drugs and would always be a drug addict—and passed out. We took our wreck of a daughter home.

Two days later, I was on a plane with Kelly back to San Antonio—we wanted to make sure she would get there. When we arrived at her barracks, she went into the sergeant's office and then I went in to talk to him alone. I was so embarrassed. He told me that if she had another AWOL, she would be out. *I was gob-smacked!! She was getting another chance??* Doug and I were sure Kelly would be "out-processing" five minutes after she arrived. When I saw all the other soldiers there, I knew she wasn't cut from their cloth. I realized it was only our hope that put her there. I walked out about thirty minutes after arriving and flew home with a bad feeling. When I got home, Doug wrote her this letter:

DEVIL'S AVATAR

Oct. 6, 2005

Kelly,

Some thoughts from Dad.

We want to help you. We can't do that unless you want to be helped, want to live. Life doesn't work in the extremes; too much of anything rots away one's soul. You seem to believe you can live this way but all your experiences there have been a disaster. Consider what you have lost:
- *your health*
- *your college education*
- *years of your life*
- *your car*
- *friends*
- *lots of money*
- *computer*
- *lots of personal property*

And you are on the edge of losing us. Continue the extreme behavior and you guarantee that will happen. Life isn't as hard as you insist on making it. As I've told you before, quit digging the hole deeper, you will never get out.

Regarding your future, I still don't know why you have to get out of the Army. It's not like you have anything better to do with yourself. You can get yourself better in the Army just as you can outside. The Army gives you a job, a role in life, pay and a sense of worth. After you get out you will need to find a job and your experience and education will only land you a low-paying job. Your freedoms will be limited—little different from the Army, really.

Chapter 10

I just don't get it. You want out so you can do what, exactly?

Please do some things for yourself:
  - call Tony
  - call other recovering friends
  - call Dr. Jay.

Please do this for us:
Go to the chapel on Sunday. Listen and you may find some help there somewhere. I don't know what it will be, but know there is something there for you if you listen.

Love,
Dad

Kelly started going to an Army psychiatrist and was diagnosed as bipolar and put on additional meds which really had her emotionally flinging around. She called us often to complain how she wouldn't get out of bed (and nobody even made her) and was completely miserable and wanted out of the Army.

While we nervously waited for Kelly's bipolar medication to kick-in soon so it could turn her life around, we researched the disorder on the internet and read books about it. I didn't have to read very much before I realized my brother and at least one uncle were definitely bipolar and some other relatives might have been.

My brother's manic-depressive behavior was always written off as resulting from a head injury he received falling down the cellar stairs when he was eight years old. He was sad (sometimes suicidal) and self-conscious all the time except, every-so-often, he would shock us with exuberance and pluck—like the time he enrolled in the University of Arizona to take courses in advanced science and mathematics. He had been out of Junior College for years and never exhibited an aptitude for either discipline. He dropped out within a week and then became too depressed to even try to get a partial refund. Though he died young of a heart attack, I believe he actually burned-out from melancholy.

My uncle, who was German, had his bipolar behavior blamed on an infection of the cerebral cortex during WWII, although he served in the rear echelons and never saw combat nor had a head injury. He was a brilliant university student who could speak several languages but amounted to little. He had several failed marriages, was alcoholic, couldn't hold a job, would blow any money he ever did have on grandiose flings like taking taxi cabs from northern Germany to Frankfurt, and, in the end, was institutionalized. Yet nobody in my family recognized this pattern of behavior across the spectrum of relatives; it was always blamed on an environmental mishap rather than heredity.

After only a few weeks of trying to adjust to the new medication, Kelly took off on her third AWOL. This time her roommate called us and told us she went to her boyfriend's place in Portland, Oregon. That was Devin, who by that time had a job in Portland and had moved from Tucson. We called him and verified that Kelly was there. We talked to Kelly; she told us she had gone AWOL on purpose to get out of the Army. We told her that was no way to do it and that she would have to go back and get kicked out the proper way—which would be much more painful than if she had asked to get out because of her mental problems. She didn't want to have to live a life

Chapter 10

looking over her shoulder and worrying about getting arrested, so she agreed to go back. We got her a flight and, this time, Doug met her at the Dallas airport to escort her back to Texas. It was his turn to be embarrassed.

Here is the letter Doug wrote to her company commander after he sent a letter informing us of her AWOL status and before we knew that she was in Portland :

October 25, 2005

Dear Captain Jones,

Thank you for your letter dated October 17th regarding the situation with our daughter, PVT Kelly Snow. Her behavior is shameful and a great embarrassment to our family.

We will assist in her return to Ft. Sam Houston to face the consequences of her actions when she reappears. She has not yet contacted us. Given her mental state when she ran off, our intent is to first get her to the hospital to continue the mental health care she was receiving before she left.

We do not know why she left. Our last contact with her was in a telephone conversation the evening of Saturday, October 15th. She was not at all well emotionally, but gave us no indication she might go AWOL. Previously she told us that she was confused and extremely depressed. This is not typical behavior for Kelly and we were very worried about her emotional well-being, which seems to have gone downhill since arriving at Ft. Sam Houston. She told us that a psychiatrist at the mental health clinic diagnosed her with bi-polar disorder. That diagnosis and the medications recently prescribed to her (Wellbutrin and Depakote), may provide some explanation for her irrational behavior. I'm not offering excuses for her actions, but want to ensure that all medical factors are taken into consideration when determining her fate.

We regret the time and effort you and your unit have expended in dealing with our daughter's actions and wish to see this situation brought to the required conclusion.

Sincerely,

Douglas Snow

(Again, as I write this, I am trying to put myself back a few years and imagine myself reading the above as a person who knows nothing of the screwed-up world of addiction. I would be thinking, "These people are too much! They tell their daughter not to disclose some of her past and join the Army then, when things go wrong, they act like she deserves what's coming to her." But, now, I would just say, "Okay. Not their proudest moment, I'm sure. But I should try walking in their shoes before judging." When you are in a ditch and there is only one rope to grab, you grab it.)

Doug took Kelly back to face the consequences of her third time being AWOL, and she was placed in the mental hospital in Fort Sam Houston. Doug stayed for several days while they tested her and gave her treatment until someone searched her purse and found the butt of a marijuana cigarette in it. Two Army Criminal Investigators promptly showed up and she was shipped off to Fort Sill, Oklahoma, to out-process with an "other than honorable" discharge. Ordinarily that would be a horrible albatross

Chapter 10

for a young person, but in her case it didn't matter. She didn't have a college degree because she couldn't manage to attend classes regularly, and she couldn't work for the same reason. She was scatter-brained, had bad credit at this point, was certified AD/HD and bi-polar, was loaded up with prescription medications, and was an illegal drug addict. Which meant that we were scraping up money to get her into another rehab.

Before we could even discuss what would come next, Kelly told us. Devin was going to come to our house with his car and a U-Haul trailer to take her up to Portland, with all of her things. I finally "lost it." I ran from our house down to the garage crying like a baby because, for me, this was the end of the line—a first taste of the end of hope. No good had come from Kelly's association with Devin before and there was no reason to think Kelly would get off illegal drugs and have some semblance of a normal life without proper treatment.

Kelly argued that she already knew what rehab was about and that all we ever wanted to do to her was put her in institutions ranging from summer camp to the Army. She knew that she had to work the Twelve Steps, avoid triggers (i.e. things that made her think about using drugs), hang around with sober friends, and see a psychiatrist to get her meds. She argued that Devin didn't take drugs because he had to go to work and that he loved her and would help her stay clean. And—she insisted—there was nothing we parents could do about it, anyway, since she had already made up her mind.

Devin arrived with the U-Haul and the two of them cleared out Kelly's room, taking all the file cabinets, journals, art supplies, collage clippings, and even her guinea pig. We hardly had a recent photo left of her, they made such a clean sweep. We hugged them both—after all, our daughter's fate was tied up with him now—and they left.

CHAPTER 11
The Roller Coaster Years

Until the last two months of her life, Kelly stayed in Portland. She loved it there. When she first arrived with Devin, she really did intend to get sober and make a new start. The problem was always the same—she never could and never would muster up the monumental effort and hard work required to do it.

I can't really write with great detail about that time, since we only saw Kelly once a year around Christmas and, even then, never for more than five days, at her request. I can tell you that no day went by for the next five years in which Doug, her grandmother, and I didn't worry about her, feel sad, and try to think of a plan of action or pray for help. Just like Kelly had "triggers" making her want to use, we had our own "triggers" taking us out of our everyday routines and constantly reminding us of our sorrows.

One such trigger for both Doug and me was seeing any girl around Kelly's age. It made no difference what she looked like; if she was normally functioning we were envious. Initially this would happen when we saw a student, bank teller, soldier, shop girl, or a girl doing anything Kelly might have been doing, and—later—it would be just a girl driving a car or speaking clearly. If the girl appeared to have low self-esteem and act like a drug user, then we only grew more sad. In my case, if the girl was with her mother and the two appeared happy together, the worse the pain would be for me. Later on in Kelly's last two years, seeing a baby would stir these emotions in us—seeing a young family was another stab. I don't begrudge all girls Kelly's age—or babies, for that matter—I'm just saying that being reminded of Kelly hurt.

Certain songs would also bother me. "Strawberry Fields Forever" by the Beatles, which I used to like, started to make me angry—there isn't anything wonderful about drugs, period. Louis Armstrong's "What a Wonderful World" was ruined for me, but I have a feeling that happens to a lot of people who encounter the down or dark side of the human condition.

I dreaded bumping into acquaintances while shopping or doing errands in our small town—especially ones I knew through Kelly. Inevitably their first inquiry would be about how Kelly was doing. I would actually hide from them in other aisles. I just didn't want to stammer my lame pre-planned answer: "Oh, you know, I haven't heard from her in a while. She's still up in Portland with her boyfriend and will probably come home for Christmas." That would usually do it for most people and allow them an ingress to tell me all about Kelly's peer—their kid—who was graduating from college or getting married or promoted, etc. Again, I don't begrudge them anything; I simply avoided reminders of how things could have been.

Chapter 11

The Roller Coaster is UP, 2006
(Kelly is 21)

Kelly's new job as a hostess in a waffle house was short-lived. She found a Portland psychiatrist who had her on six different medications for bi-polar disorder, ADD, sleep disorder, and whatever. He said exercise would help her, so we bought her a fitness club membership—which turned out to be a waste of money since Kelly was usually too depressed to go. She was a complete basket case on all of that medication and called me crying every day before she was to show up at work. We told her to hang in there and keep trying with the meds to get the right mixture, we tried to explain that it takes time. We had to believe prescription drugs were better than illegal ones.

Kelly went back to school, this time at Portland Community College, to try the waters again. She took three "soft" classes. One of them was stand-up comedy and she was thrilled. My mom and I drove up to see her that March, and told her she could have our old car because we were getting a new one. Before we gave it to her, we called her L.A. psychologist for advice and he said it was a good idea. We found it strange that her old psychologist still kept in contact with her. We told her we would pay him to help her, and she said not to because he was her buddy. *That's nice, makes no sense, but it's nice, we thought.* Her apartment in Portland was tidy and clean, Kelly was nicely dressed and she and Devin were happy together. My mom and I flew back to Arizona with some hope.

Good thing we had learned not to let our hopes get high, because the pain from the downhill roller coaster ride always hurt too badly. Kelly stopped going to all the classes except for comedy. This all resulted in more thrown-away tuition and books; we were used to this by now. I don't remember much about the rest of 2006, except that we gave Kelly and Devin tickets to Cancun from airline miles and, for Christmas, another set of flights home to see us. We didn't see a lot of Kelly; she spent most of the visit in Tucson at Devin's family's house. During that visit, we met Devin's parents, who were very nice people. Still there was something about Kelly that made us think she was using again because of her remoteness towards us.

The Roller Coaster is DOWN, 2007

Sure enough, by springtime, Kelly was hanging out with a new guy while Devin was at work. She told us Chase was both Devin's and her friend and he was a college student living in the dorm. According to Kelly, Devin spent most of his free time playing computer games with his geek friends, which left her bored. Of course, we all know that idle hands are the Devil's workshop. I got a bizarre phone call from Kelly one night—she was high as a kite and asking me if I could give her some potential names for a guinea pig because Chase was going to get one to be friends with hers. *She was how old??? How old was he?*

We knew she was relapsing. We also knew that we couldn't keep on supporting her (at that time, we were paying for her medical insurance, car insurance, doctor bills, medicine, storage bill, and phone). We decided to buy a cabin in the White Mountains of Arizona, which would lock up our money so we couldn't let it drain away on rehabs that didn't work for Kelly. Plus, I remembered

Chapter 11

the older couple from Valley Hope who told me that was how they stayed sane, and thought it would work for us, too. We took a trip up to the mountains, found a cabin, told the realtor we would buy it, and called Kelly on July 5th to tell her what we had done.

Kelly knew she always had a standing offer from us that if she really wanted to go to a rehab, we would pay for it. This new plan would just make it harder to do and, thus, would make us be sure she was serious and really meant to do the hard work before we paid that much money ever again. The first words out of Kelly's mouth before I could even tell her our good news were, "I need to go back to rehab." She was using cocaine along with alcohol, prescription meds, marijuana, and other "stuff." Devin's mom was a psychiatrist, and personally recommended Kelly go to the Schick Schadel clinic in Seattle for electric shock treatment.

So much for "our life." We called the realtor and cancelled the purchase of the cabin. Then we called him back and uncancelled. *Dammit, we could not let Kelly destroy our lives.* The shock therapy was something new. Maybe they could shock Kelly out of drugs. (Honestly, I hoped they would shock the shit out of her so she would finally snap to.) Kelly intimated that she and Devin were engaged and that they needed this to work. Maybe this new reason to stop the drug abuse, combined with a new type of treatment, would be the answer. We would have tried anything at that point. We paid the $15,000 for ten days, and I went back to "Mom Bank."

The electric shock therapy was a really big mistake. It was a sham. The obvious appeal to Kelly was the lack of effort it required on her part. All she had to do was become a passive recipient, take the shocks, and "voila" problem solved. We should have known better. How could we have fallen for something like that?

A few days after the shock clinic, Kelly left Devin in a mean way. When he came home from work one day, all her things were gone. She had not even left him a note. Chase had helped her move out and into his dorm. A few days after that, Kelly over-dosed on cocaine. My mom happened to be visiting me when I got the call from a girlfriend of Kelly's. She said Kelly was in Chase's dorm room when it happened and he ran her out to the curb and dumped her, and then ran back up to his room to flush away the evidence. Strangers had to call 911. *The avatar was being slammed around.* Maybe the Devil was trying to have a "two-fer" and cause my mother to have a heart attack as well. I talked to the doctor on the phone, who told me they had to defibrillate Kelly's heart, but that she was okay.

Contact with Kelly stopped after that—there were no answers to our calls. By December, we somehow got a hold of her and offered her a flight home. We were so worried; we wanted to see what she was looking like those days. She tried to get us to give Chase a ticket, too, but finally she agreed to come home alone. She was 95 pounds and on drugs when we picked her up from the airport, although her usual weight was about 115.

We could have picked up anybody's kid from the drug park and had the same quality visit. She had no interest in us, our home, or our pets. We took her to see the new cabin—no interest, either. She told me, later, that the reason we had to stop so many times at convenience stores on the trip up and back to the cabin was so she could buy little shots of alcohol and triple-strength coffee and Red Bull, not really because she had to go to the bathroom.

Chapter 11

When she visited her grandmother in Tucson, she stole drugs from her bathroom. She visited Devin, who was also home in Arizona with his family for the holidays, and with Miles—who was on leave from the Army. The less time she spent with us, the better she seemed to like it. Of course, all the time she was telling us how well she was doing and how she wasn't using drugs anymore, except for marijuana. She was so loaded that even her significant lying skills had deteriorated.

Before she left, Doug asked her to do us one favor: write her name and our phone number on a piece of paper and keep it in a pocket so that we'd at least be spared the cruel fate of never knowing what happened to her.

Nothing She Does Can Surprise Us Anymore, 2008

We lost contact with her for the next five months. Her phone number no longer worked and neither did Chase's. We decided that was the time we would be forced into trying "tough love" since we couldn't reach Kelly, anyway. Everyone told us to do it; so there it was. We later learned that she and Chase lived on the street and in a garage. The only payment we kept making was her medical insurance, because we feared she would overdose and end up needing extreme medical care, which could wipe us out since we wouldn't say "no" to it. We had no idea how she got money to live, except we began to get "robo calls" at our house from debt collection agencies, which gave us some idea. (We haven't stopped getting them since.)

We went up to our new cabin, but just brought our sadness along with us. So much for an escape from our pain. The cabin had a whole closet full of toys and children's clothing left behind by the prior owners. We bagged all of it up and donated it to a charity shop; we would never be grandparents—there would never be grandchildren to take fishing, skiing or hiking. (We already knew it back then.)

This was also the time when my mother developed a fascination with Lindsey Lohan, as if she could keep track of whatever was happening to Kelly by watching the celebrity news about Lindsey. I would get calls to "quick turn the T.V. on" to catch Lindsey going into or out of a rehab. My mother's pain of imagining her only grandchild on the streets could only be shared with Doug and me. Mom would tell me every single time she called that we needed to fly up to Portland and put Kelly in a mental institution. But, even if we could have found her, I don't know how we could have put an adult—who didn't want to go—into an institution. We would have had to kidnap her. She wasn't a threat to others, and her biggest resentment against us as her parents was that we were always trying to institutionalize her. We thought that if we could just have gotten her to come home, we could have dealt with her from there.

During that same time, I was doing a lot of kneeling at my windowsill and praying. One day I realized that I was not really praying, I was just begging, so I decided to show the Lord that I was not a "one trick pony." I would demonstrate to him that I actually knew some proper prayers. First I prayed the new one I had learned, the Serenity Prayer, and then the old one from my childhood, The Lord's Prayer. For the first time, for me, it wasn't just rote recitation—I actually realized the prayer contained everything I had learned so far about the Twelve Steps and I realized that it provides a way for us to navigate through the human condition.

Chapter 11

"The Our Father Prayer"
(Roman Catholic version of the Lord's Prayer)
Our Father, who art in heaven,
Hallowed be thy name;
Thy Kingdom come
Thy will be done
On earth as it is in heaven.
Give us this day our daily bread;
And forgive us our trespasses
As we forgive those who trespass against us;
And lead us not into temptation,
But deliver us from evil.

"Our Father, who art in heaven, hallowed be thy name" tells us to recognize and honor our higher power (Steps 2 and 3 of the program). The next lines of the prayer are Step One of the program; they tell us that nothing is for sure—everything is God's will and you aren't in control of things (i.e. you're powerless): "Thy kingdom come, thy will be done, on earth as it is in heaven." They emphasize to addicts in rehab to just worry about making it through each day and take one day at a time: "Give us this day" and to let God sustain us literally and figuratively "our daily bread" (Steps 11 and 12). And then there is the forgiveness part (4th through 10th Steps). You can't move on saddled with baggage, you need to forgive others—and yourself—to get a clean slate. Otherwise, you're like an overweight person who gobbles down another candy bar because it simply doesn't matter when you are that far gone. But, if you are at a good weight, then eating the next candy bar *does* matter. Likewise, if you are off of drugs and "clean," then risking relapse by soiling yourself with a drug or a drink *does* matter.

DEVIL'S AVATAR

In Kelly's case, I believe she saw herself as having transgressed so far that she might as well have kept going, since she felt she was irrevocably tarnished. She worked through the Twelve Steps, but couldn't grasp the first two lines of the prayer: she couldn't connect with God. Unfortunately, for the Twelve-Step program, that MUST happen or the rest won't help.

The last line of the Lord's Prayer is self-explanatory about keeping evil and temptation away from us. Note that the prayer begins with God ("Our Father") and ends with the word "evil." These two opposing primary forces of the universe, good and evil, bracket the prayer like they bracket our lives—constantly pulling and pushing. (Wow, all that time we were paying rehabs and psychiatrists when The Lord's Prayer was free counseling therapy from God himself. I don't think Kelly knew The Lord's Prayer. I have made such a terrible mistake raising her.)

The first call from Kelly in five months woke me up on Mother's Day at five in the morning. I was secretly hoping she would call me that day, but I wouldn't let myself be hurt if she didn't, so I tried not to expect anything. However, when it came in at such a bizarre time, I already knew she would be drugged-out. Kelly was so high she was rapid-firing her words. She told me she had had a revelation and that God has talked to her and cured her from drugs and she wanted to share this wonderful news with me on Mother's Day. She said she had just buried her last drug underneath a tree. She was going to be clean from then on. This hurt so badly on Mother's Day. She wasn't saying it to be mean, she was so high that she actually believed it. That was the Devil making light mischief with his avatar; he was saving the real evil for the next month.

Chapter 11

In June, after hearing nothing for so long, we got panicked calls from Chase, who was drunk, or, loaded asking me to do something about Kelly because she'd "gone crazy." Then Kelly called to give me the "good news" that I was going to be a grandmother! She said she was two months pregnant and had only had one slip-up two days before when she over-dosed on heroin and was hospitalized and maybe the day before that when she got messed-up with some OxyContin, but, aside from those two mishaps, she just wanted me to know the good news. I told my girlfriend many times that nothing Kelly could do would surprise me anymore, but I didn't see this one coming.

We called Dr. Jay and he called Kelly and talked her out of going through with the pregnancy. He tried to explain that the baby would be so messed-up it wouldn't be right to do this. Kelly called me two days later and asked if we would pay the $450 for the abortion because she was going camping that coming weekend and wanted to get rid of the "kid." The Kelly we knew would never have said a thing like that. The Devil now had complete control of his avatar. Kelly was no longer putting up any resistance. (In the end, it turned out she didn't need an abortion, the fetus was "reabsorbed" or something like that.)

Doug had sent a letter to the people in the garage earlier in the year (I forget how we found the address) where we last knew Kelly and Chase had been living, asking them to pass it on to Kelly. It was returned to us in July along with the following letter from a girl who knew her:

Dear Mr. Snow,

Here is the letter that you sent. I don't know where to find her anymore. To be honest I really didn't care. I consider myself a compassionate person and she even pushed me past the point of caring.

The only reason why I am writing you back is I feel you and your wife deserve to know what is going on. I don't know if Chase can bring himself to be objective about the matter. He does love her. But, she is out of control. She IS going to kill herself and her baby. My recommendation is to come to Portland, pick her up, and bring her home until she has her baby. Maybe there is something you can do.

We tried to help her, we couldn't. Also, I don't know if she told you but she overdosed on heroin and was clinically dead until the paramedics arrived. They revived her with CPR and some kind of chemical to make her heart start again.

I am in nursing and what I would recommend is to file to become her power of attorney. She is not capable of helping herself. (Do not send her cash.)

God Bless,
R. I.
(former roommate)

No more news came from Kelly until October. We learned that, during the time that passed, she had neglected her car to the point it could no longer be driven and she left it for impound. Her driver's license was revoked. She wanted to know if we would pay for an apartment for her and Chase because she was going to get a job at a bar and wanted to turn her life around. She asked if we would pay for her to go to bartender school in order to get a job. We didn't care anymore that bartending isn't a

Chapter 11

good idea for an alcoholic, we just heard the word "job." We just wanted her to support herself and so we paid for a bartending school. It sounds stupid now, but at the time we wanted anything that even resembled normalcy and earning some money. I actually remember saying, "If you can't beat them, join them."

She wanted to come home for Christmas, but wouldn't come unless Chase could come, too, because "he was going to be in her life forever and we might as well accept it." We gave them tickets, because we needed to see Kelly again. Before she came home, she needed $2,000 worth of periodontal work because her gums hurt her. (I guess when you're homeless and drugged-out you forget to brush your teeth.) We had spent thousands on her braces, so we weren't going to let all her teeth fall out and further hinder her for when she actually turned the corner and came around to living a normal life. (Yes, we thought that maybe she would still mature. Somewhere I had read that it takes some kids until 25 years old. We still had two years.)

Their Christmas visit was actually wonderful. Kelly looked so good, like we hadn't seen her look in years. She had gained weight and looked healthy. She had finally stopped the vegetarianism (which I still resent for having caused so much havoc in our lives)—through necessity since she had to eat what she could get. The two of them drank some beer—but not in excess—and didn't act like they were high or appear to be on drugs at all. And by then, I knew how to tell. They took hikes and rode horses. It made us very happy to see them together like that.

We even liked Chase, which I wasn't prepared to do. Our new nicer selves have helped us understand that people's lives can go wrong and, before they know it, they can be in a tailspin. Chase is another kid who went off the path and got himself mixed-up with drugs; we knew from our long experience with Kelly—it happens. He had ended up in prison for five years. He became the black sheep of a good Mormon family and was ostracized. When he met Kelly, he was trying to finish up his degree and climb out of his ditch. It wasn't easy, because he was almost blind from a genetic disorder. Kelly is not the woman you need to meet when you are trying to straighten out, but she was magnetic. Indeed, the overdose incident at his dorm got him kicked out and back at ground zero. I did tell him I still held resentment against him for throwing Kelly out on the curb, but he said that was not the way it happened. Was that the truth? Lies? I stopped trying to figure it out. Everyone in the world of drugs lies. I was just happy that—for the moment—everything seemed to be going well.

We watched Chase as he helped Kelly by providing the common sense element for the relationship. He reminded her to take her sweater, not to leave her purse or lose her keys, etc. That was the level at which Kelly couldn't function, even though her wit and higher reasoning were intact. Her lack of common sense required a "minder" or Kelly could never function. The problem was that her boyfriends always started out as "good-time Charlie" party friends. At some point, when the boyfriend began to love her and want a future with her and began truly caring by trying to help her stop doing drugs, Kelly would find a new boyfriend who was still in the good-time Charlie party phase of a relationship. This was a pattern that had repeated itself through Miles and Devin, and it was about to happen to Chase.

Chapter 11

We Can Still be Surprised, 2009

After Christmas, we didn't have a lot of contact. We were angry at Kelly most of the time for losing cellphones and she seemed to only call us when she needed a new one. We were tired of buying them for her, but we kept doing it so that we would know where she was. Her voice was slurred almost every time we talked to her. She would tell us how great she was doing at comedy and that her career was about to take off. We told her she was sabotaging her comedy routine because nobody could even understand her.

One call I made to her found her slurring and crying. Her "friends" had stolen a Target gift card I had given her out of her purse when she went to the bathroom. A normal person would wonder how she could call people who would do such a thing "friends," and why she didn't take her purse to the bathroom with her like every other woman. This was the curse of her having no common sense—a curse magnified on drugs. Over and over again people would rip her off, abuse her, and take advantage of her. She was like a lamb out in a world of wolves. A person like she was should not have been loose.

In June, she called and asked for money for an abortion. She said that Chase didn't know, and that they were fighting horribly. Here is where the Devil smeared me with sin using Kelly, his avatar. I am against abortion, but I couldn't see Kelly bringing an innocent child—probably deformed and maybe mentally retarded—into the world. I gave her the money. Now I have an evil sin on my conscience, too.

After the abortion, Chase and Kelly fought terribly—for a long time we got phone calls from her crying. She was a wreck. She and Chase broke up.

At some point in the summer, Kelly said Dr. Jay paid for her flight to L.A. to see him at a hotel. This sounded weird to us. Then we got a call from Chase who told me he knew we really liked and respected Dr. Jay, but that he had email evidence proving there was something hinky going on between Kelly and Dr. Jay. He said he would send me the emails to prove it, if I wanted. I said, "No." That was actually too much evil for me to handle. Kelly grabbed the phone from Chase and said he was lying because he was jealous. I began to wonder if there was anyone who could stay untouched by the evil of drugs. Kelly flew to L.A. and called us from the hotel. She said Dr. Jay had been there, but that Miles was with her and she wanted me to say "hi" to him. (It was all pretty nuts, who can figure any of this out?)

Back in Portland, Kelly camped at the summer festivals. She began using food stamps, so she rarely called us to recharge a grocery store debit card we had given her. Once when we talked to her, she said she was a "featured comedian" with her name on the kiosk in the parking lot.

In August, Chase called to say he was worried that Kelly might overdose on heroin and that it could kill her this time because she was so thin. She had a new boyfriend, Aaron, who was an actual homeless guy who shot her up because she was afraid of needles. (*Nice.*) Chase wanted us to rescue her. He said the worst thing she was taking was Adderall from her quack psychiatrist in Portland, which completely rattled her brain. He said he dreaded the days she picked up her prescription. This psychiatrist would just refill prescriptions without ever checking to

Chapter 11

see how Kelly was doing—or what she was doing. She would take whole handfuls in one swallow sometimes and, other times, she would sell some of the pills.

We called Dr. Jay and asked what she looked like when he saw her in L.A. He said she looked bad and was really "out there." He said he would try to encourage her to go to rehab from his end. We booked a flight for Kelly to come home. She canceled it (costing us an additional $100). Two weeks later she slept-in and missed her rescheduled flight (another $100). Finally, she arrived on a third flight—all in black, scrawny, back slouched, discombobulated, with a ring in her nose and having lost her phone in the airport toilet. Things fell out of her purse as she ran back and forth to the baggage turnstiles all confused.

In the car I told her she needed to eat. That elicited mumbles and tears. She told us that Aaron's mom loved him and accepted him for who he was and she wanted to know why we couldn't accept her for who she was. She said that was all she wanted from us. I told her, "Of course we love you, but we will never accept you being a drug addict. Never. We wouldn't be good parents if we did that." This resulted in more mumbles and tears.

At some point in the conversation, Kelly nonchalantly tossed in the extra information that Aaron's mother was a witch. When she told me that, I didn't say, "Kelly, what the hell are you doing? Look at the type of people you're hanging around with: Witchcraft-mother, heroin-injecting homeless boyfriend—what are you thinking?? STOP IT!" It's hard to explain to someone who hasn't been through the addiction nightmare, why a mother wouldn't say SOMETHING—or do ANYTHING. But I didn't. I just sat and listened as if we had been having a completely normal mother-daughter chat. You come to a point where you know nothing you say will matter—nothing you do will matter. You reach a point of acceptance of the disease. We rarely saw her. I didn't want to fight. I was beaten down.

When we arrived home, Doug had a nice dinner ready for us and Kelly managed to shock us with her table manners. They were like an animal's—elbows on the table, hunched over, fist around the spoon, mashing the food, throwing and spitting parts out. We couldn't understand what had happened. *When did that happen? Who was that person?*

The first thing she did was to find Miles, whose time in the Army was up and he was getting ready to be discharged. He had been wounded more than once in Iraq and now had PTSD (Post Traumatic Stress Disorder). He was always trying to save Kelly, even then, when his own plate was full. We told Kelly to leave him alone. He didn't need to be messed-up by her. But Miles would never abandon Kelly and she would always call him because she knew he would be there.

My mom had not seen Kelly in two years because of the incident when Kelly stole medications out of her bathroom, so I set up a meeting between them. Kelly dressed in a classic whore outfit: skimpy clothes all in black with a red camisole on top.

In the car on the way she dumped out her feelings toward me: She wished we had three children so she could be the middle kid—the one left alone—not pestered. She wondered why we couldn't accept her just the way she was and appreciate her accomplishments, like her comedy routines. She accused us of never making her do chores, which didn't help her to become independent. (At which point I reminded her that she wouldn't listen, learn, care,

Chapter 11

help, be interested, trusted, or depended upon.) Then she told me that rehab screwed her up; it was the worst thing that ever happened to her in her life. And then I learned about her rape, when she ran away to L.A. She said that her discharge from the military was our fault and our idea and—as we approached her grandmother's house—she lashed out saying that I had poisoned her relationship with my mom. The visit with her grandmother was a disaster.

When I took her back home she didn't even want to spend the night with us. She said we were boring and our house was cold. Doug asked why she even came to visit. "You made me," She snapped. After that, we never even broached the subject of putting her in a mental hospital. We knew she would never agree and would just hate us even more. We told her to get off of whatever drugs she was taking, because they were rattling her brain. Either that—or nine years of drugs—had taken its toll.

Every phone call for the rest of the year had a drugged-out slurred Kelly on the other end.

CHAPTER 12
The Dark Year, 2010

In February of 2010, we got a collect call from jail. Finally she could check that box off of her list—we all knew it was coming. It seemed she had gotten arrested for shoplifting two months earlier and hadn't shown up to fulfill her community service. I went online to see exactly why she had been arrested, because I couldn't believe anything she told me anymore. When her mug shot popped up, it felt like a spear had just been thrown out of the computer screen and into my heart. You can be intellectually prepared for something, but still not emotionally. I kept staring, trying to believe I was actually seeing Kelly's face—that it wasn't a mistake. She was sentenced to thirty hours, but—in classic ADD style—she had only done eleven, causing her to have to spend six nights in jail. I actually wished her jail time had been longer—long enough for her to get clean. At that point I saw jail as a forced refuge from drugs. (How could it have come to the point where I wished my daughter would be in jail—because it would be a "good" thing?)

DEVIL'S AVATAR

After she got out, I talked to her on the phone and she sounded like her old self again, except for an up-tick in dishonesty. Still, it was amazing what six days of no drugs did for her. She really hated jail and said she would never do anything to put herself in there again. She told me she was drunk with some friends when she stole some tops from a Sears store in Portland. (How I hated the lies! She was no doubt on crack cocaine and heroin as well as alcohol. "Drunk" was simply a euphemism she used with us, because she knew how much we hated her drug use.) I asked her why she stole when she knew we would have helped her for things like that. She said she was so glad she was not on that "other stuff" anymore. (More lies.) Meanwhile she said she owed Sears $300 and asked if I could give that to her. (Still more lies.)

In April, she called to say she was getting kicked-out of her apartment, because the road was being widened and the building was being torn down—forcing everyone to go. (We found out that these were more lies—she was personally being kicked out.) She was still working hard on comedy and was on the brink of making it big. (More lies.) She still had her part time job at Starbucks, which she jokingly called her "corporate job." (Lies, lies, lies!) The Devil wouldn't be able to keep his avatars captive if he just used chemical dependency alone. He has to use a fog of lies to hide his handiwork.

Moreover, once you have become an avatar, there will eventually come a time when the Devil will want to exit your body. When that time comes, there are four different ways he can do it:

1. He can screw-up your mind, but leave your body intact. (A very cruel fate, because the Devil will park you

Chapter 12

in a mental institution and leave you—you'll no longer be any fun for him.)

2. He can get your body arrested by the police, but leave your mind intact. (Also a very cruel fate. He will only get out temporarily until you use substances again.)

3. The Devil can just crash land you and climb out of his avatar because it is dead. (This is his favorite way out and he sees to it that the majority of his avatars stay in an intoxicated stupor until the time comes for him to make his exit.)

4. Or, you can kick him out. (Very difficult to do, because you are his hostage—tied-up, drugged, and gagged in his cargo hold—within your own body!) But you can call out for help from inside of your head. You just need to understand that you have unwittingly gotten yourself mixed-up in a primal war between the forces of good and evil. You will have to acknowledge the fact that you are powerless and pick the side you want to be on. After you have chosen the side of good, you will need to get as close as you can to God and let good and evil fight it out. That's what they do—eternally. Your job is to cling tightly to God's side for safety; this fight is bigger than you.

I realize it is an old message, but it was new to us, at least the way it was delivered—fresh, hard, and personally. I wanted to tell Kelly, but I feared she was so far gone, she might misinterpret what I was saying about good and evil. I didn't want her to think I was insinuating that she was bad. I never thought that. If you knew her, you knew she was a good person and meant to harm no one except herself, which is the case, from what I have learned, with most drug addicts. She made bad decisions, got herself hooked and the ditch digging began. She never stopped digging and ended up with an overwhelming excavation the size of the Grand Canyon *in her mind.*

I should have at least tried to tell her that I knew what was going on and that she could still climb out of her ditch. I wrote some letters to her, but threw them away telling myself that Kelly needed to make the trip into God's grace on her own. That's how it works; your mom can't do it for you. Still, rather than just praying for God to help her, she deserved to hear the message clearly from us. Add another regret to the big pile. I can only ring the bell for anyone else who would benefit from hearing it: Addiction is a process of usurpation. The fight for freedom takes place on a higher plain.

Another month passed and we didn't hear from Kelly. So, one day, I just "out-of-the-blue" went on the internet to the Portland jail website and did a search, and up popped a new arrest photo of Kelly. There she was—she looked awful, like the deterioration photos of addicts you see at county buildings in order to scare young people away from using meth. Listed with her photo were eight felony counts. I couldn't understand the acronyms but they looked like drug dealing. I called the 24-hour line and an official translated the acronyms for me. They included: meth and marijuana possession and dealing, magic mushroom possession, manufacturing, dealing and some other type of mushroom and LSD dealing.

My girlfriend told me I should look up the creepy boyfriend, Aaron, to see if he was arrested, too. Sure enough, there he was with the most heart-stopping blood-chilling mug shot. He had two charges: one for harassment and the other with $10,000 bail for strangulation!!! Kelly's charges were eventually dropped, but he remained jailed.

Chapter 12

The strangulation charge was from a while earlier, when he had tried to kill his stepfather.

We immediately contacted a three-month rehab in Tucson and, while we were in the process of trying to get Kelly to come home, Miles's mother, Lana, called me saying that Miles was dead. He had died in their home while Lana was in Iraq (where she worked as a civilian for the military). This was such terrible and incomprehensible news. All I could think about was how differently the dominoes of Miles's life could have been set up had he never met Kelly, had he never gone in the Army, had he…. (There should have been so many more dominoes in his chain when it toppled. He was only 24 years old.)

Lana and her daughter wanted Kelly to be at his funeral. We got her home immediately and she showed up at the airport acting "normal." We were sure Miles's death would cut through to Kelly. After all, he was her oldest and best friend. He was the one true friend she could call any time and he would be there. She said his death was a "game-changer;" she said she didn't want anything to do with drugs again and was glad Aaron was in jail so she could break away from him. She gave a clear and coherent eulogy for Miles in church during the funeral. Her hair was up neatly and she looked like a "regular girl" in her cardigan and skirt. We noticed her posture had improved; I didn't have to tell her to stand up straight once. I liked it that Kelly had never gotten a tattoo; neither had Miles, come to think about it. Lana remarked that Kelly seemed to have "made it." Kelly even hung around with us parents for the first time on a visit. We were happy that Aaron, the strangler, was in jail and couldn't bother her anymore. *May he rot in there.* She wanted to rent a room with a girl for a change and begin dating. She said she would go to a rehab if we insisted, but she wouldn't stay and we'd just be wasting our money. We let it drop, because we had learned that unless a person wants rehab, it will not work. Maybe Miles's death had an impact and she really would change.

As soon as she got back to Portland, the strangler had been let out and they were back together. We pleaded and begged for her to get rid of him. Her friends all pleaded, but it was no use. They had an intervention for her to no avail. A few days later, we were sent the bill for damages to the apartment she had been living in when she was arrested—$1,600 and photos to prove it. They showed that it was completely trashed—even spray paint on the walls. Doug said "never again" would we co-sign a lease and I could have said that I had told him not to do it the last time, but I felt we didn't need to start fighting among ourselves.

(Never could I have imagined, back in those heady days when I ignorantly thought Valley Hope was a dorky name for a rehab, that we would come to profoundly understand its meaning. Even more unimaginable to me is that, in only a few years, we would have traveled all the way across the Valley of Hope to a far place of no return on the other side. We had somehow ended up PAST hope. Looking behind us, I prayed we could have one last chance in the valley, but we knew in our hearts that that time had passed.)

After Kelly was back in Portland, she and the strangler rented rooms in different houses—and got evicted from each one—until August when Aaron's uncle gave him a break and said he would teach him plumbing in Stockton, California.

Chapter 12

In September, Kelly was supposed to move there so they could live together in a little house in a cornfield as "normals"—happily ever after—and make a baby. Unfortunately, she hated Stockton and Aaron's uncle—and I'm sure the feeling was mutual. After crazy stuff like stealing the uncle's van and driving around in it without a license, running away on a Greyhound to Portland, seriously injuring her foot, not sleeping for six days, being so loaded Chase had to put her in a wheelchair (because she could hardly walk) and then on a plane back to Stockton, etc., Kelly literally begged us to get her out of there. She hated her situation in Stockton and wanted to "reconnect" with us. We translated that to "I'm out of money and out of options." She called us collect and said she and Aaron were so broke that they picked up all the cigarette butts around the truck stop she was calling from and smoked them (this is true because I read it in her final journal). She asked if I could wire her $50, finishing up her request with "Please, Mom?"

(When your daughter is little and you have dreams of what she'll be when she grows up, could you even imagine her drugged-out and picking up other people's cigarette butts from the ground and smoking them with a strangler boyfriend? Where is the doctor boyfriend? Where is the lawyer? Forget that, where is the day laborer? Anybody else? How did it get this bad?)

We got her on a plane and had her back with us the by the last week of October. Kelly was limping and wearing ratty clothing, but I was relieved that she didn't look like her police mug shot in real life. For a person who had so badly mistreated her body with almost ten years of drugging and lack of sleep, she was still pretty, although she was starting to look older than her 25 years. Hard living was catching up to her; we could tell there had been a decline. I offered to buy her new clothes and shoes, and even to get her hair done and—for the first time ever—Kelly had no interest. I knew something was really wrong!

Kelly and I had a horse ride (our first together in years), because each time she had come to visit us before, she had ridden with her boyfriend. I, at least, thought we were "reconnecting" when, after two days home, she announced that Aaron was at the Tucson Greyhound Station and wanted me to give her a ride there. I told her he was never setting foot in our house—and that she was not to even think that. She told me I should just drop her off so she could be with him.

I put our two old bicycles in the back of the truck so that they could get around Tucson and drove her there. When I saw him at the Greyhound Station, I didn't know what to do. How could I drop Kelly off, with no money, to be homeless with this creep? He was hungry, so I bought them lunch and decided to put them in a motel for two nights until I could go home and talk to Doug about what to do.

This time it was I who asked Doug if we could pay the rent for them for just one month and see if it was true, if Aaron really would get a handyman job and Kelly really would get ANY job. They both swore to me in the truck when I took them to the motel that they had come to Tucson to start over. Aaron said his uncle gave him a good reference and that he had common sense and could help Kelly; he would cook for her and take care of her. I actually wanted to hear that someone would help Kelly—completely blocking out the fact that Aaron is a certified strangler (not to mention scary-looking). *What else could I do?* The alternative at that point was to walk away from

Chapter 12

our daughter forever, a step that Doug and I knew was coming and dreaded. Kelly said they wanted to be married and I might as well accept him.

During the same truck ride, Kelly also told me that she was "born to smoke" and that she would never stop smoking marijuana. Then she began crying and, when I asked her why, she said, "I'm afraid you will be mad and disappointed in me if I ever relapse." What she was saying—but what I wasn't hearing—was that she wasn't planning on quitting drugs, she was so hooked that she *couldn't* quit drugs.

I drove back to Tucson two days later to pick them up from the motel and to find them an apartment. "Never again" turned into "one last time" when I signed for a three-month lease. We set them up with food and gave them money to get access to the internet. The first month went by and neither of them got a job nor managed even to get the internet going. We decided to allow Aaron to come over to our house for Thanksgiving—against every fiber in my body—because we wanted to see Kelly and she wouldn't come without him.

On the day before Thanksgiving, I drove with my girlfriend to pick them up. I called Kelly three times to be sure she would be ready when we arrived to pick them up. When we got there, Kelly was drugged out of her mind, sitting on the floor trying on some clothes from a huge pile of cast-off clothing she said they found by a dumpster. I could barely understand her, but she said Aaron wasn't there because he was downtown buying marijuana. *Right!* Then she suggested that we pick him up on the way. *How far gone would your brain have to be to say that to your mother? Sure! I'd gladly pick up your strangler boyfriend, honey, from his drug deal and take him home so I can feed* *him a nice turkey dinner!* I was so disgusted, I said, "You know what, Kelly, f*ck Thanksgiving dinner with you!" and went back to the car and drove home. Those were the last words I ever spoke to her.

Doug talked to Kelly on the phone one more time a few days after Thanksgiving about ringing up a $300.00 telephone bill on the cell phone we had loaned her three weeks before. To say the least, our communication with Kelly in those weeks was not very congenial. On December 11, Doug and I were planning to go to Tucson to check on Kelly after not hearing from her for almost two weeks. But, early that morning, we received a call from the police telling us that she was in grave condition at St. Joseph's Medical Center. When we arrived, the doctor told us that Kelly wouldn't make it and that she had really done a whammy on herself as they rarely see an overdose like hers. She had heroin, cocaine, amphetamines, and a whole list of other things in her system.

The doctor said her corneas were "blown," her lungs were seeping, her kidneys were in failure, and that the only reason her heart was beating was because of some large dose of a type of heart drug they gave her. She had been brought to the hospital way too late. There was no mention even of organ donation; everything was ruined. The strangler boyfriend, although only a block away, never came to the hospital. In the end, it was just our little family huddling together in the Intensive Care Unit—we stayed together through thick and thin, with each other despite it all. The Devil's joy ride in our daughter's body was over; he was out.

Doug and I felt guilty, because when her heart finally stopped and we looked at Kelly lying there quietly, we both felt the same thing: a sense of relief for her tortured

Chapter 12

body and soul. We realized that no one could hurt her anymore; she couldn't hurt herself anymore. The frenzy in her head had at last stopped. It was like when she was little, except this time the crazy party was over for good and all the reveler-friends had been sent away forever and Kelly would never wake-up again after being sent to bed.

My mother held my hand to console me and expressed the same general feeling, telling me that Kelly was "safe."

It took me a long time after Kelly's death to finally understand what my mother had said. I had to let it marinate for a while and think, because "safe" was a strange way to describe a twenty-five-year-old, who has just died. After all, you never see the word "safe" printed in sympathy cards. Usually a person is considered to be "safe" if she manages to stave off death. In Kelly's case, though, she was finally "safe" from her life, which the hobbles of addiction had demanded be led as an ignoble Devil's avatar. She had hated every minute of disappointing her friends, family and herself, and no longer had to worry about that.

Finally we had a sensible answer to our perpetual question of "why?" Why would a person so beautiful, smart, personable and beloved treat her life so cheaply? The question is perplexing unless you answer it from the inside out. It took us all that time to finally understand, because Kelly had been using thick layers of jokes, laughter, and comedy to entomb, barricade, and conceal unfathomable tragedy. When Kelly would come home to see us—her dorky parents living their unchanged quiet middle-class lives—we must have been like unwitting mirrors to her. She probably didn't want to have to look at her own reflection, because that would have meant her carefully hidden pain of who she had been and what she could have been would begin to bubble up and stir, threatening to poke out through its dark encasement to remind her. I'm sure when she avoided us as much as possible, it was her way of fighting back. We always just assumed she didn't like us, though we never understood why. Our constant efforts to help probably only made her feel worse, since she knew they were all futile.

It took me until writing this to unravel the riddle of the bad posture she had had for all those years. Why, I wondered, did it improve in the last year? What happened to her during that time? The answer, I believe, was heroin. Once she was on it, Kelly cared about nothing else and went into her final descent, which was an all-out freefall. No more conscience—no more posture problem; there was no more shame or guilt anymore to pull her down. It was as sad and as simple as that.

Miles's mom, Lana, came over to see us right away after Kelly died. We commiserated as only people who have gone through losing a child can do. One question vexed us the most: Why is it that some families, no matter how dysfunctional, manage to have all their children leave the nest and all of them end up successful or at least doing okay? How was it that our kids were dead, even though we actually tried to be good parents and give them safe and good homes? We didn't get it.

Two days later after Kelly's death we went back to Tucson to make sure Aaron left the apartment. We wanted him to just go away. He was crying, and Doug felt sorry for him and allowed him a week to get out. For a twenty-five-year-old person, Kelly had hardly any possessions.

Chapter 12

She had lost her wallet, identification cards, most of her jewelry, and anything of value. We took home some files, some collages, her favorite belt buckle, a notebook of new joke ideas, and her last journal. We went to the funeral parlor next, and told the mortician to write down "comedian" for Kelly's occupation on her death certificate. We thought she would have liked that. Less than a week before Christmas, we drove up to Tucson, again, to pick up her remains. They handed us what looked like a shoebox wrapped in silver paper complete with a tag—something that looked like a Christmas present. We didn't have any emotions left to think about that.

Back at home, I read Kelly's last journal, which we had brought home from the apartment. I had to read it, because I couldn't stop wondering whether Aaron had strangled her. His story to the police was that they had drunk a bottle of Tequila together and "crashed" at 4 AM. He woke up at 6 AM to go to the bathroom and found her unconscious and cold, at which time he called 911.

Since the death was from drug overdose, the body had to undergo an autopsy. The coroner determined her death was caused by a stroke. The toxicology report showed levels of both cocaine and heroin at five times higher than her body could tolerate. There was no trace of alcohol. I will wonder to my last day if Aaron waited too long before he called the police because he was scared, or for whatever reason.

I don't even know why we bother asking lying avatars questions about what happened, anyway. We should probably just ask the Devil himself, but he is very busy these days.

CHAPTER 13
Leftover Evil

It was the end of December before we were able to get into Kelly's apartment to clean it. When Aaron left, he gave the keys to a homeless man and his dog that pooped all over the carpets. We walked in on the guy and threw him out, but the mess we were left with was disgusting. How can an apartment get that gross in seven weeks? Who knows how many drug parties were held in there?

We found butane (for sniffing?), pills, marijuana and alcohol. The toilet had a note on it telling people not to flush! They must have been hiding their stash in the tank. Satan really had a last blast before his avatar crashed. We worked all day cleaning and still would have to forfeit the deposit. Doug found a weird greeting card in the middle of the carnage. It was from Aaron's mother. The front had a drawing of a young fantasy couple in Medieval/Middle Earth clothes. The girl had pointed ears and was holding a chalice, preparing to drink. The young man, also with pointed ears, had his arm around her while he was blowing a hunting horn. On the inside left of the card was a line drawing of a pentagram with what looks like a glitter smear on it from his mom.

Aaron's mother wrote (I've transcribed it here exactly as it was written):

Aaron,

I had saved this card to send to you and Kelly, I knew she would have "digged it."

It reminded me of you and her. You blowing your horn to let the world know she was yours and you were hers. And she carries the chalice the elixir of your undividing love for each other.

I decided to send it anyway, thou she is gone in body, she will always be with you in spirit. When you feel that cool breath on your neck. She is reminding you she is near.

Love,
Mom

Doug and I just looked at each other with disbelief. *Who ARE these people?* I wanted to throw it out quickly, but Doug said to save the card. Who knows? If I ever wanted to write about what happened to Kelly, it would all be part of the story. Indeed, he was right. The Devil, having finished his play, left us his condolence card.

CHAPTER 14
Finding the Files

While reading the one journal I did read, Kelly's last, my heart broke all over again. Ninety percent of Kelly's entries were about drugs, i.e. how much she loved them, who gave her what, what she took, how great it felt, etc. Drugs were her everything in her last days.

In one entry, she wrote that she wanted to have a baby to make up to God for her two abortions. I think Kelly also saw her friends getting clean and leaving drugs behind when they had kids and she thought that would be a way for her to do it. Doug and I wondered if the pressure to have a baby (however irresponsible that would have seemed to a normal person) was a factor in her all-out drug bender towards the end—knowing that once she was pregnant she wouldn't be able to take drugs anymore.

So many drugs were described in her journal that I could see her handwriting becoming correspondingly more scribbly four weeks before her death. At two weeks out, she stopped writing all together. She went into an all-out freefall. I believe if there were drugs stronger than heroin, she would have taken them, too, in excess. In fact, I am sorry I even read her last journal, because it has left me with an indelible mental image I can't seem to shake. I think of a lab rat that has learned to push the lever for drugs and—within a short time—no longer cares about anything but frenetically working the lever for more and more and more.

Knowing how hopelessly addicted Kelly was and how final death is, as we do now, I can't help wondering if we were wrong in not accepting her as she was. I've heard of a rock star, who has been addicted to heroin all his life and has a doctor "manage" the size and quality of his dose. Why wouldn't that have been an option for Kelly? We were just adamant about insisting on no drugs. Every conversation ended with us telling her to just get off of drugs. When it became evident that she would never be able to do that, why didn't we just take her any way we could get her?

After thinking this over, we realized that we had, in effect, already accepted a certain level of Kelly's addictions. We accepted that she would never stop smoking marijuana, as she told us many times. We accepted she would be an alcoholic and even paid for her to attend bartending school (which her ADD rendered worthless). In effect, we were trying to make a deal with the Devil. But you can't "deal" with him—he will win. The problem for Kelly was always the same: no amount of anything would ever be enough—a "maintenance dose" would be impossible. The only way to "deal" with the Devil is to expose him by casting light on the evil wrought by his poisonous drugs.

Chapter 14

We know the Devil is behind our daughter's ruined life and premature death.

We know that he uses drugs as poisonous bait for weakened and troubled individuals.

We know what he does with their brains and bodies—how he uses them to spread Evil.

We're onto him.

We're exposing him.

We know Evil.

The accordion file we took from her apartment told its own story of a person in decline but still, pathetically, trying to grapple with her problems and pull her life together:

> *1st slot: Apartment forms and info; scrap paper with jokes*
> *2nd slot: Medication warnings for Adderall (a prescription drug for bipolar disorder); newspaper clipping of people in Mardi Gras costumes*
> *3rd slot: Nutrition guide; warning pamphlets for inhalants; "Problem with drugs? Want Help?" pamphlet; her hospital wrist band from her last overdose; pamphlets on pregnancy, the dangers of Marijuana and help for quitting smoking*
> *4th slot: A post card from a dentist saying she missed her appointment; two mailing envelopes; prescription info for Clonazepam; a Methamphetamine fact sheet; job search websites; a pumpkin-carving book*
> *5th slot: Greyhound ticket stubs; another wrist band from a hospital overdose;*
> *a prophylactic; paper about laws affecting cancelled checks*

*6th slot: A Halloween card I had sent her; blank paper;
a "to-do" list: get toothpaste, name kitties*

CHAPTER 15
Trip to Portland

Doug and I flew up to Portland to get Kelly's things out of a storage unit and to reclaim her computer from the police impound (where it had been since her drug arrest). Chase had told us he and some of Kelly's friends were going to hold a memorial for her on the 8th of January, so we decided to combine all of that in a three-day trip. We stayed in a hotel where Chase's family was staying. We didn't realize they were going to do it, but Chase's parents and brother drove all the way from Utah to attend Kelly's memorial and support Chase. They hoped this would be a time of change for him, as we did. We liked his parents very much and could tell they had been through a lot just as we had been. It only took us seconds to feel the connection. There was that tell-tale fatigue—minus all the judgment.

We got all Kelly's things out of a downtown Portland storage locker and brought them up to our hotel room to sort through. All that was left of Kelly's earthly possessions were two large files, seven collage posters, a plastic tub of sentimental junk, some old clothes and, of course, her fifty journals. What to do with them required some contemplation.

For a kid who began life with everything, this was all she had left. She probably had to bite her lip to call us all those many years and ask if we would pay the storage bills—usually with late fees. These were the final things that meant something to her. The tub of junk made us cry. There were things in there that we couldn't believe she had kept: a little wooden screw-top box with her milk teeth from the tooth fairy, retainers from braces, a little wallet from the Parent Banc that vexed us so much when she couldn't grasp the concept of money, lots of broken jewelry, single earrings, little keepsakes of a life of fun and good times. There was a little National Park passbook that she carried on all of our trips to get it stamped. Broken trinkets, all, but all must have had sentimental value to survive to the point of our hotel room floor.

Chase came to our room and we gave him Kelly's file on him. We told him we knew of two overdoses she had before her final one. He held up four fingers to correct us, and then he confessed to us something that was deeply bothering him. He said he felt guilty because when he learned Kelly had died, he felt a relief for her. We told him we had the same guilt; we felt the same way.

That evening, Doug and I spent several hours going through the tightly stuffed filing cabinet, throwing away papers that we didn't understand or wish to understand. The point was to just carry back with us on the plane the important things. The idea of filing must have given Kelly a sense of order to her otherwise chaotic brain. There were files on everything from "mischievous behavior" (traffic tickets, faked checks, etc.), files with pamphlets on the

Chapter 15

dangers of drugs, notes to herself about stopping drugs, notes in the next file about how great drugs were and how much fun, a file on religion and churches, etc.

It was all so hard to understand, because Kelly started her life out with the world as her oyster: she had looks, brains, a good home, loving parents, world travel, ponies, cars, etc. We couldn't understand why she never once complained to us about not having a car anymore or nice clothes or a computer, since she was used to having all those things. But she didn't. Kelly was down to nothing but files, journals, and a box of junk. All these years it was hard for us not to help her as we could easily have given her many things. We kept our help just to the basics—food and shelter—so she would have to work towards the rest.

Some files made us laugh because they reminded us about Kelly's sense of humor and what great fun she was. Others we threw out immediately as we really didn't want to know that she did the things they represented. There was also a shoebox of photos. Most pictures were of people we knew when she was younger and all were happy except there were five black and white photos of her and Aaron from a time of decline. They were shoved into her happy life of photos just like he shoved himself into her real life at the end. He never belonged—just like those five photos didn't belong. If she hadn't been a drug addict, she would never have even looked at a guy like that. We tore the five photos up. I couldn't look at the guy.

The computer we had returned to us from the police impound came with a warning from the officer that it contained some things we may not want to see. We appreciated the warning, because we *didn't* want to see. Doug shoved a screwdriver into the hard drive and smashed it.

I wish all the bad memories in my head could go away as easily.

We didn't know what to expect at her memorial. Luckily, we learned that Aaron wouldn't make an appearance. He took a Greyhound to Portland to go to the memorial but was shunned by all of Kelly's friends as *persona non grata* and left town. A pavilion was rented in an arboretum and about thirty people attended—including Devin—in spite of 36-degree drizzling rainy weather. Many of them stayed to stand around for three freezing hours.

Her friends spanned all walks of life. We had no idea how many friends Kelly had! She told me she had her own transformation through living a hard life into a person who finally stepped out of herself and put others first. I had had trouble believing her, but here was the proof! Our strained relations with Kelly had kept us from knowing who she was and appreciating her. How many times did she tell us that she simply wanted our acceptance of her just as she was? Yet that could never have happened. We were her parents and we could never have accepted her drug abuse—which would have been tantamount to not loving her.

Chase and his mom had made a collage of Kelly's photos. Someone else brought a smiley face balloon and let it float away. Kelly was always smiling.

CHAPTER 16
A Final File, January 2005

I found the list, below, in Kelly's files from early January 2005, when she first came back home after being kicked out of the Herbert House and before she tried the Army. After I read it, I realized everything in LIFE made Kelly want to use. We had no idea that this was what she was going through. It has opened our eyes to what horrors must be going on inside the hearts and souls of other addicts.

WHY I WANT TO GET HIGH

1) it would greatly reduce my craving to get high
2) I enjoy the euphoria
3) I'm rather idle
4) I am very unaccustomed to being sober at this house
5) my nerves would receive great relief from stress
6) it isn't a big deal unless I make it one
7) I like to hallucinate
8) I miss being in my parallel universe

---

9) because I am totally not supposed to
10) it is a favorite social pastime
11) reality is boring
12) I'm feeling self-defeating and in sabotage mode
13) I like to snort stuff
14) it's easier than saying no
15) things are more exciting distorted
16) it's DANGER
17) DANGER gives me a rush
18) enhances any activity
19) I get to keep a secret stash
20) I'll be back in on the big "inside joke" that brings users together the way AA does
21) to prove that the world is not lost to me
22) now I don't walk around in fear and suspicion of being triggered to get high and losing my sobriety
23) temporary relief of never ending problems
24) my pictures are more aesthetically pleasing and inspired
25) my friends are more fun, even if I'm the only intoxicated one
26) I might have a really far-out good idea (while high) that could improve reality
27) it feels good

THINGS THAT MAKE ME WANT TO USE:

1) the bright yellow military science station light at the top of the end of the mountains at night
2) ceiling fan
3) my room after 8 PM
4) Scott Evil (Kelly's guinea pig)
5) bathroom floor tiles
6) my computer
7) family dinner
8) anxiety about not being able to quit after a little

Chapter 16

9) anxiety about not being able to quit in the first place
10) journal thoughts
11) my bed
12) any music
13) trippy concepts in books like the string theory of parallel universe talk
14) my old pictures/paintings
15) bright; flashy; colorful lights
16) anything boring
17) being too tired
18) being too awake
19) making difficult phone calls
20) trying to draw, paint, or write
21) most movies
22) movie theater
23) airport
24) grocery store
25) anything sociably fun, e.g.: bowling, mini golf, theme park
26) disappointment, rejection
27) Wal-Mart and Hastings (a book, music, and video store)
28) Venice Beach
29) my old job
30) every ex-boyfriend, ever
31) lethargy
32) sick days
33) vacations
34) walking around, hiking
35) my friend, Miles
36) my car
37) watching TV/movies with my parents
38) traffic
39) Taco Bell food
40) 420-anything, tripper toys

41) using scenes in movies
42) That 70's Show
43) speak of partying/ using
44) everything on cartoon network
45) a. Christmas
b. Thanksgiving
c. Halloween
d. Easter
e. New Year
d. Earth Day
46) my birthday or anyone else's
47) my grandma
48) Bisbee, Arizona
49) Any anxiety about anything
50) speak of subconscious thought, the transference of human consciousness, irregular brain activity, symptoms of psychedelic use in general

25 THINGS THAT MAKE MY LIFE UNMANAGEABLE BECAUSE OF USING

1) credit card debt
2) kicked out of house (Herbert House)
3) Mom and Dad don't trust me
4) more therapy
5) quit school(s)
6) quit job
7) lost Yeem's friendship
8) compulsive eat/buy/fuck habits
9) can't party
10) MOOD.
11) have to stay away from my best friend, Miles
12) can't remember any significant events/conversations/people/etc. between 2001-04
13) need medication
14) rejected by sober friends/peers

Chapter 16

> *15) dishonesty*
> *16) obsessing about using all the time*
> *17) many manipulative using boyfriends*
> *18) destroyed parents/their finances*
> *19) permanently hallucinating*
> *20) have to be "monitored" by sober living therapists, UA, etc. constantly*
> *21) lost $$ thousands in drugs*
> *22) cost almost $100,000 in one year of rehab*
> *23) anxiety/stress of holding secrets*
> *24) unmanageable paranoia of getting found out*
> *25) aged my body*
> *26) missed 3 years of unretainable knowledge, even though I sat/worked through schools*
> *27) made friends' parents warn them about me*
> *28) eternal rehab relapse rehab relapse ……*
> *29) moved indefinitely around 10 times in about a year*

DEVIL'S AVATAR

> *The message I would deliver to my (past)-self if I could transport my (present) self back in time:*
>
> *(Back to High School graduation) Quit while you're ahead, drop the losers/stick with the winners, get the Fuck out of your home town and apply yourself to U. of A. Don't do anything you wouldn't want to be caught doing on a hidden camera at home. (and for the love of life, Kelly, don't touch crystal Meth with a 100-foot pole)*

References

Twelve-step program
A twelve-step program is a set of guiding principles outlining a course of action for recovery from addiction, compulsion, or other behavioral problems. Originally proposed by Alcoholics Anonymous (AA) as a method of recovery from alcoholism, the Twelve Steps were first published in the book, Alcoholics Anonymous: The Story of How More Than One Hundred Men Have Recovered From Alcoholism in 1939. The method was then adapted and became the foundation of other twelve-step programs. As summarized by the American Psychological Association, the process involves the following:
- admitting that one cannot control one's addiction or compulsion;
- recognizing a higher power that can give strength;
- examining past errors with the help of a sponsor (experienced member);
- making amends for these errors;

- learning to live a new life with a new code of behavior;
- helping others who suffer from the same addictions or compulsions.

Overview

Twelve-step methods have been adopted to address a wide range of substance abuse and dependency problems. Over 200 self-help organizations–often known as fellowships–with a worldwide membership of millions, now employ twelve-step principles for recovery. Narcotics Anonymous was formed by addicts who did not relate to the specifics of alcohol dependency. Similar demographic preferences related to the addicts' drug of choice [have] led to the creation of Cocaine Anonymous, Crystal Meth Anonymous, Pills Anonymous and Marijuana Anonymous. Behavioral issues such as compulsion for, and/or addiction to, gambling, food, sex, hoarding, debting and work are addressed in fellowships such as Gamblers Anonymous, Overeaters Anonymous, Sexual Compulsives Anonymous, Clutterers Anonymous, Debtors Anonymous and Workaholics Anonymous. Auxiliary groups such as Al-Anon and Nar-Anon, for friends and family members of alcoholics and addicts, respectively, are part of a response to treating addiction as a disease that is enabled by family systems.

History

Alcoholics Anonymous (AA), the first twelve-step fellowship, was founded in 1935 by Bill Wilson and Dr. Bob Smith, known to AA members as "Bill W." and "Dr. Bob", in Akron, Ohio. They established the tradition

References

within the "anonymous" twelve-step programs of using only first names "at the level of press, radio and film."

As AA was growing in the 1930s and 1940s, definite guiding principles began to emerge as the Twelve Traditions. A Singleness of purpose emerged as Tradition Five: "Each group has but one primary purpose—to carry its message to the alcoholic who still suffers." Consequently, drug addicts who do not suffer from the specifics of alcoholism involved in AA hoping for recovery technically are not welcome in "closed" meetings unless they have a desire to stop drinking alcohol. The reason for such emphasis on alcoholism as the problem is to overcome denial and distraction. Thus the principles of AA have been used to form many numbers of other fellowships for those recovering from various pathologies, each of which in turn emphasizes recovery from the specific malady which brought the sufferer into the fellowship.

In 1953 AA gave permission for Narcotics Anonymous to use its Steps and Traditions.

Twelve Steps

These are the original Twelve Steps as published by Alcoholics Anonymous:

1. We admitted we were powerless over alcohol—that our lives had become unmanageable.
2. Came to believe that a Power greater than ourselves could restore us to sanity.
3. Made a decision to turn our will and our lives over to the care of God as we understood Him.
4. Made a searching and fearless moral inventory of ourselves.

5. Admitted to God, to ourselves, and to another human being the exact nature of our wrongs.
6. Were entirely ready to have God remove all these defects of character.
7. Humbly asked Him to remove our shortcomings.
8. Made a list of all persons we had harmed, and became willing to make amends to them all.
9. Made direct amends to such people wherever possible, except when to do so would injure them or others.
10. Continued to take personal inventory and when we were wrong promptly admitted it.
11. Sought through prayer and meditation to improve our conscious contact with God as we understood Him, praying only for knowledge of His will for us and the power to carry that out.
12. Having had a spiritual awakening as the result of these steps, we tried to carry this message to alcoholics, and to practice these principles in all our affairs.

In some cases, where other twelve-step groups have adapted the AA steps as guiding principles, they have been altered to emphasize principles important to those particular fellowships, to remove gender-biased or specific religious language.

Wikipedia, s.v. "Twelve-Step Program," http://en.wikipedia.org/wiki/12_step_program (accessed July 27, 2011).

References

ADD/ADHD in adults can cause forgetfulness, distractions

By Mary Ackerley, MD, MDH

(from The New Southwest (Tucson), December 2010)

Adult Attention Deficit Disorder is not well known or recognized, yet it is estimated to affect more than four percent of the population. However, only 10 percent of that population is actually being treated for the illness.

Characteristic symptoms of ADD include impulsivity, easy distraction, disorganization, forgetfulness and inability to perform tasks requiring sustained concentration. Restlessness, or hyperactivity, does not have to be present to make the diagnosis. One of the easiest ways to make the diagnosis is to have a child diagnosed with AD/HD, since ADD appears to be highly genetic. In fact, it is usually when the child is brought in for treatment that it becomes obvious one of the parents also share the diagnosis.

Adult ADD is a very common cause of marital strife, financial problems, job failures, drug abuse, felonies, traffic accidents and low self esteem, which is why diagnosis of AD/HD in adults is important. Recent studies have found that approximately 50 percent of felons have ADD. Untreated ADD sufferers have a higher incidence of motor vehicle accidents, speeding tickets, citations for driving without a license and suspended or revoked licenses. More than 50 percent of untreated teens and adults abuse alcohol and drugs.

People with ADD typically have problems doing routine, unexciting tasks. Oftentimes they procrastinate or never finish a project. Many times people with ADD will say, "I can pay attention – as long as I am interested."

DEVIL'S AVATAR

This plays havoc with keeping jobs or running households. People with ADD often have erratic work histories despite being quite bright and often creative and innovative. Most employers will not tolerate missed deadlines and unfinished projects. At home the problems continue. Although the majority of ADD sufferers are men, about 15 percent are female. Partners of ADD sufferers frequently complain that they get to do everything "that's not fun" which usually includes disciplining the kids, remembering their appointments, handling all the finances, including making budgets and keeping records, organizing the household, including finding lost items, and in general being the "grownup" in the relationship.

SPECT scanning is a brain imaging technique which can show the brain's activity. Dr. Daniel Amen, a psychiatrist and Assistant Clinical Professor of Psychiatry and Human Behavior at the University of California, Irvine School of Medicine, has shown that many ADD sufferers have low activity in their prefrontal cortex. The prefrontal cortex is the "executive" of the brain. Involved with planning, impulse control and decision making, this cortex is not fully developed until the mid-20s in most people. That is why children need parental supervision – they lack the brain capacity to fully understand the long term consequences of their actions, and the discipline to not act on impulse alone.

The prefrontal cortex allows one to make goals and achieve them in the absence of external structure. This is considered to be an essential aspect of a mature and effective personality. In many people with ADD this center shuts down the harder they try to concentrate, which is seen as an inability to focus and pay attention. It also creates poor impulse control. Often, in stressful situations, people will think thoughts that are better not said, such as "You idiot. A person with an IQ of 10 could have done a better job." Most people realize that saying such thoughts will only make the situation worse. However, a person with ADD often lacks the ability to censor his thoughts, blurts out whatever he is thinking, and escalates the situation or argument.

Successful treatment for adult ADD involves recognition, first of all, of the problem and then acceptance of the diagnosis. Most other people around the patient recognize the problem before the patient does, although they may not know what to call it. The employer and the spouse may both recognize that the adult ADD sufferer cannot be depended on for being on time, for finishing project, for paying attention to details or for paying bills. Employers deal with it usually by firing the employee. In the marital situation the relationship troubles may simmer for years without treatment. Many marital counselors are actually treating ADD relationships, often without recognizing it. There are many questionnaires on the Internet for diagnosing ADD. One that is useful is Dr. Amen's (www.amenclinics.com/cybcyb/onlinetests-calculators/add-test). It should be noted that the online tests are screening tests only and a professional confirmation of the diagnosis should be obtained.

Once the diagnosis is obtained, treatment is essential. Successful treatment has several components.

The first, again, is accurate diagnosis and overcoming denial. Many do not move beyond the denial, preferring to believe that their behavior is not a problem. Often this comes from low self-esteem. By the time an ADD patient reaches adulthood he or she has endured extreme amounts of criticism from parents and teachers. Often s/he has internalized the idea that s/he is lazy and dumb. Actually, admitting finally that there is a real problem simply adds to the poor self image, and the person finds it easier to ignore the message, and perhaps to try to kill the messenger, who is usually the long suffering spouse.

However, effective treatment does exist and it is highly worth obtaining. The most effective treatment programs consist of psychological interventions, exercise, diet, nutritional supplementation and medication.

Author: Dr. Mary Ackerley, MD, MDH, is a classically trained psychiatrist and homeopathic physician in private practice in Tucson.

References

Bipolar disorder
Manic depression; Bipolar affective disorder

U.S. National Library of Medicine
National Institutes of Health

Bipolar disorder involves periods of elevated or irritable mood (mania), alternating with periods of depression. The "mood swings" between mania and depression can be very abrupt.

Causes, incidence, and risk factors
Bipolar disorder affects men and women equally. It usually appears between ages 15-25. The exact cause is unknown, but it occurs more often in relatives of people with bipolar disorder.

Types of bipolar disorder:
People with bipolar disorder type I have had at least one fully manic episode with periods of major depression. In the past, bipolar disorder type I was called manic depression.

People with bipolar disorder type II have never experienced full-fledged mania. Instead they experience periods of hypomania (elevated levels of energy and impulsiveness that are not as extreme as the symptoms of mania). These hypomanic periods alternate with episodes of depression.

A mild form of bipolar disorder called cyclothymia involves less severe mood swings with alternating periods of hypomania and mild depression. People with bipolar disorder type II or cyclothymia may be misdiagnosed as having depression alone.

In most people with bipolar disorder, there is no clear cause for the manic or depressive episodes. The following may trigger a manic episode in people who are vulnerable to the illness:
Life changes such as childbirth
Medications such as antidepressants or steroids
Periods of sleeplessness
Recreational drug use
Symptoms

The manic phase may last from days to months and can include the following symptoms:
Agitation or irritation
Inflated self-esteem (delusions of grandeur, false beliefs in special abilities)
Little need for sleep
Noticeably elevated mood
Hyperactivity
Increased energy
Lack of self-control
Racing thoughts
Over-involvement in activities
Poor temper control
Reckless behavior
Binge eating, drinking, and/or drug use
Impaired judgment
Sexual promiscuity
Spending sprees
Tendency to be easily distracted

These symptoms of mania are seen with bipolar disorder I. In people with bipolar disorder II, hypomanic episodes involve similar symptoms that are less intense.

The depressed phase of both types of bipolar disorder includes the following symptoms:
Daily low mood
Difficulty concentrating, remembering, or making decisions
Eating disturbances
Loss of appetite and weight loss
Overeating and weight gain
Fatigue or listlessness
Feelings of worthlessness, hopelessness and/or guilt
Loss of self-esteem
Persistent sadness
Persistent thoughts of death
Sleep disturbances
Excessive sleepiness
Inability to sleep
Suicidal thoughts
Withdrawal from activities that were once enjoyed
Withdrawal from friends

There is a high risk of suicide with bipolar disorder. While in either phase, patients may abuse alcohol or other substances, which can make the symptoms worse.

Sometimes there is an overlap between the two phases. Manic and depressive symptoms may occur together or quickly one after the other in what is called a mixed state.

Expectations (prognosis)

Mood-stabilizing medication can help control the symptoms of bipolar disorder. However, patients often need help and support to take medicine properly and to ensure that any episodes of mania and depression are treated as early as possible.

Some people stop taking the medication as soon as they feel better or because they want to experience the productivity and creativity associated with mania. Although these early manic states may feel good, discontinuing medication may have very negative consequences.

Suicide is a very real risk during both mania and depression. Suicidal thoughts, ideas, and gestures in people with bipolar affective disorder require immediate emergency attention.

Complications
Stopping or improperly taking medication can cause your symptoms to come back, and lead to the following complications:
Alcohol and/or drug abuse as a strategy to "self-medicate"
Personal relationships, work, and finances suffer
Suicidal thoughts and behaviors

This illness is challenging to treat. Patients and their friends and family must be aware of the risks of neglecting to treat bipolar disorder.

excerpts taken from: http://www.ncbi.nlm.nih.gov/pubmedhealth/PMH0001924, accessed March 21, 2010